SHOOTING SCRIPT

Also by William Tremblay

Crying in the Cheap Seats
The Anarchist Heart
Home Front
Second Sun: Ideas of Order in Little Canada
The June Rise
Rainstorm Over the Alphabet

SHOOTING SCRIPT

poetry by

Bill Tremblay

EWU
P·R·E·S·S

EASTERN WASHINGTON UNIVERSITY PRESS

SPOKANE, WASHINGTON

Cover design by Scott Poole
Book design by Joelean Copeland

ACKNOWLEDGEMENTS

Some of the poems in this book have appeared first in the following
literary magazines: "A Night on the Town," *Green Mountains Review*;
"Hollywood Comes to San Angel," *Massachusetts Review*; "A Dream and
a Waking," *Spoon River Poetry Review*; "Leon's Love Letter to Frida,"
Manoa: A Journal of International Writing of the Pacific Rim; "Pyramid
of the Sun" and "Noche de Niños Muertos," Soundings East;" "The
Writing on the Wall" in *CeReBuS*; "Dream of an Afternoon," in *ZZZ
Zyne*; "Diego Drives Leon to Cuernavaca" and "The Blue House," in
turnrow; "Diego Shows Leon the House," "Actor Without A Script,"
"Frida Renders the Mock Trial," and "Diego Voice-Over: Mirror of
Night" in *Seattle Review*; "Burning the Judases" and "The Writing on
the Wall" in *Louisiana Review*.

I would also like to thank the friends who helped me fashion this book
into its present form: Floyce Alexander, James Bertolino, Nancy Baxter,
Mary Crow, James Grabill, Christopher Howell, George Kalamaras, Ted
Lardner, Deanna Ludwin, Jack Martin, John Clark Pratt, Christopher
Robé, and Bonny Barry Sanders.

Library of Congress Cataloging-in-Publication Data

Tremblay, Bill.
    Shooting script : door of fire : poems / by Bill Tremblay.
        p. cm.
    ISBN 0-910055-91-2 (alk. paper)
    1. Trotsky, Leon, 1879-1940--Poetry. 2. Breton, Andrâe,
1896-1966--Poetry. 3. Kahlo, Frida--Poetry. 4. Rivera, Diego,
1886-1957--Poetry. I. Title.
    PS3570.R38S55 2003
    811'.54--dc21
                                        2003014683

Table of Contents

For Cynthia,
mi compañera, without whom this book could not have
been written.

To love life with open eyes, with a critical spirit which never surrenders, without illusions, never embellishing it, but always taking it as it is, for whatever it may have to offer us, and even more for what it may become—that is an achievement of the highest order.

—Lev Davidovich Brohnstein
a.k.a. Leon Trotsky

What is a film but an animated mural? Light expands three-dimensionally through a hundred feet of space in a darkened theatre. It re-assembles, in two dimensions, on a screen. The montage completes itself in the minds of the audience.

—Sergei Eisenstein
summarized from *Notes of a Film Director*

The Blue House

Evening. Pan down a herringbone sky
the color of hammered copper, sunbeams
through royal palmfronds striking the indigo walls
Diego painted as a wedding present to Frida,
giving it a fountain for a mouth and a tongue of water
so it could bear its blue witness.

A slight breeze stirs *papier maché*
Japanese lanterns like penny-banks holding
echoes of soirées where Mexico City's wild angels
gathered to sing with tequila throats
and raise a glass to the door of fire.

On the terrace Diego, in 20 gallon
white Stetson, Frida in denim workshirt,
slump like rag puppets on wrought-iron chairs.
Indio workmen on scaffolds batter out
street-side window frames with six-pound sledges,
the blows, their echoes, trochaic, unbearable,
rock the walls that stand like an open sarcophagus,
cradling bamboo gardens aflame with Birds of Paradise.

Other workers brick up holes,
turn the hacienda to a fortress to give their guest
the exile asylum from the assassins everyone knows are coming.
She raises her head to ask:—*Why clean house for a dead man?*
Diego lifts his bulging frog-like eyelids:
—*To appease your mother's ghost.*
Frida sees a third eye on his forehead, closing.
She hoists herself up with her ivory cane:
—*Time to bury the magic of the house.*

As she hobbles toward the garden
she is seen though the film of a self-portrait
in a *gallería* window. In the *retablo* she sprawls,
naked, her pubic hair scrolled piano wire, the stillborn
she bore Diego orbiting the Detroit Ford factory
in a planetary system with her pelvis,
an orchid, hooked surgical tools, the painting a collision
between her suffering and her instinct for form.

Diego touches her chin:—*I must paint you.*
Frida brushes his hand away:—*Don't.*
You have Mexico. All I have is me.
He whistles loudly. Two boys in Communion suits
rush through the gate, filling her arms with blue gardenias.
Mariachis march in, silver trumpets blaring.
She lifts her eyebrow:—*Another of your desperate fiestas?*
Diego dances like an elegant elephant.
Frida waves off the street-band
with her flower scepter, hobbles back to the terrace.

In the sky above her,
a film in slow-motion: a trolley-car
crashes a bus, an 18 year old Frida spins
like a ballerina from the wreck, one giant fishhook
through her abdomen and out her vagina,
her girlhood prayers to be special answered at last.
She tilts the whiskey back:—*I try to drown my sorrows,*
        but they've learned to swim.

Water spurts from a fountain over a stone Tlaloc:
geraniums sprout from a three-legged pot
shaped like a fetus strangled by its umbilicus:
—*I will never love anoth...*
What she leaves unsaid brings him to his knees:

—After all we've meant to each other?
—I need a new inspiration, a vortex, a nebula… a divorce…
A clash of metal is workmen
shattering wine bottles, imbedding glass razors
into wet cement to scoop the knees of would-be thieves.
Pulling his head to her breasts, she whispers:—*My baby.*
He stands, plods up the staircase, stops, turns, looks back.
She is looking into sunset
stropping clouds into blood-wet knives.
What she has done is not the same as tossing away
young men like pinches of spilled salt.
A hummingbird hovers above her shoulder.
Last light glimmers over orange-tiled rooftops.
The workmen are beating the Blue House to death.
With each hammer blow, it moans.

Night Augury

Frida turns, tosses, awake
for the last time in her father's house.
She feels someone, -thing, out in the night
calling her. She limps downstairs
to the replica of the Aztec altar she had built
in the garden, lights a torch,
splits the rind of darkness open:
carved ochre masks, jaguars, serpents,
a priest-king pierces his foreskin
with a bone knife. She pulls a newsphoto
from her pocket-on the Kremlin balcony
a young Leon stands, Lenin's sponsoring hand
on his shoulder. Millions march below
in Red Square on the first May Day.
She unwraps her gauzed foot, thick clots
glop on newsprint, and, burning it
in torch flames, watches black smoke drift
to a wall of bamboo. There, a girl with glowing
jade eyes steps through, holding out
a straw basket with one leathery egg in it:
—*What of the exile?* she asks.
—*He's a dead man,* Frida answers,
breaking the egg open. A baby crocodile
slides out of clear jelly, bites her thumb:
—*Even a dead viper may give a killing wound,*
the girl says as she dissolves into smoke.
Alone. Silence. And in it all that can be heard
is the a-rhythmia of rain drops spattering
on dry azaleas. Close, on her hand,
in her palm, blood pools into a red star.

Welcome to the New World

Through the porthole of a Norwegian steamer
Leon watches morning fog rise above Tampico.
Dawn light etches ten years of hard exile in his face.
Seagulls circle above oily waters in a tightening noose.
The ship's propeller churns in his stomach,
thrush, thrush, thrush, thrush. Its engines stop
give a final thrash, jolting his knees.
He steadies himself, one hand on the wall
beside a framed photo:
    A meeting hall packed with workers, soldiers.
    It comes alive. Cigarette smoke rises. Leon enters.
    As he mounts the stage, each man pinches off
    a bit of his flesh. On-stage, a skeleton with a goatee
    makes the speech:—*Kerensky can't provide*
        the necessities of life, Comrades!
    He finds more profit in making the instruments of death!
Laughter... Darkness... Silence... A loud knock.
His wife bolts from her bunk to the WC, clutching her clothes.
The Captain's white uniform fills the doorway:
—*We're locking down the ship. You must now leave.*
The old man draws his finger across his throat:
—*So assassins can finish us on the docks?*
The doorway's suddenly crowded. Flashbulbs pop!
Leon recognizes a face:—*Alfred!*
Alfred Rosmer in Panama suit clears his throat:
—*On this historic day, here are Mexican officials,*
journalists and this lady. Frida steps forward
in her blue Tehuana dress:—*Welcome to the New World.*
Her youthful eyes gleam obsidian, their depths
rock him like a tugboat bumping the ship.

Leon's wife steps out, still buttoning, in the mirror,
Frida, a native queen; she, dissheveled, gives a hopeless shrug.
—*Where is Diego?*
Frida's eyes still fixed on Leon:—*I'm not his keeper.*
Leon kisses her hand:—*At last, to meet you.*
Frida curtsies:—*History, in the flesh.*
—*This is the last move we shall make!* his wife declares to the ceiling.
—*All but our triumphal return to Moscow, Natalia.*

Close Iris   Open Iris
As the entourage crosses a palm-treed *zócalo*
a white stone Olmec head stares at them
entering the rail station where a locomotive stands,
throbbing and hissing under the banner *El Hidalgo*.
A crowd of workers in their Sunday best
materialize through its wall of steam, singing:
—*Arise ye pris'ners of starvation,*
        Arise ye wretchèd of the earth…
Leon smiles, waves at the crowd, until a placard appears:
        GO HOME TRAITOR
His smile dissolves, he urges Natalia up the steps.
The train as it departs is painted like a strip of movie film.

Close Iris   Open Iris
A mountain pass framed by passenger windows.
A military officer stands in the aisle beside Natalia
smoking a cigarette as the train crests a summit.
Distant peaks float like schooners with snow-colored
sails, sunset tinted clouds like platters of cut-open
pomegranates. Leon asks the officer:—*Is this the route
Cortés took?*—*Yes. Moctezuma might've killed him
in these narrow defiles, but he couldn't conceive
the Spaniard as a threat.* Leon looks out his window:
four campesinos stagger up a dirt road under loads of
mesquite. Sunlight on cacti makes long crucifix
shadows in the dust like a grid the men's black humps

move across. He sees ghosts rise from dead Russian
soldiers drift like smoke across World War I battlefields.
The train enters a tunnel with a shrill blast, steam
enfolding the passenger car. In electric light, behind
Natalia's back, Leon's hand reaches. Sparks...
the voltage of Frida's thigh.

Hollywood Comes to San Angel

Diego jams a champagne bottle like maracas in a silver ice bucket.
On every studio wall, campesinos march, machetes on shoulders,
blue cacti like winnowing hands of the dead sprout from earth
to beseech the pitiless sun, peasant women in rebozos
beg alms at the gates of El Chapultepec. Doorbell chimes!
When he opens it, there stands Paulette Goddard,
a small radiant woman in white summer dress, big garden-party hat.
She hands him an envelope:—*From Gershwin.*
—*What are you doing in Mexico?* ripping the letter open.
—*A photo—shoot for Look magazine to publicize my latest comedy…*
      and Georgie says you should paint me.
Diego reads:—*He actually calls me 'a Latin lover'?*
—*Aren't you?* Paulette's eyes spark with teasing.
—*I regard the terrible virility of the men in my family as a curse.*
—*Just my luck.* She unpins her hat, lays it on a table.
—*But how shall I pose you?*
Paulette's eyes say she'll become whatever Diego imagines.
He dances her toward a wall covered in photographer's backdrop paper.
She gives him a down-from-under look:—*Was that a tango?*
Diego feels her heat, her short intakes of breath.
—*The silver screen has never done you justice.*
—*You like movies?* She picks up champagne bottle.
—*The gangster ones,* the slang they talk, it tickles me.
—*Say some.* She peels back the pink foil.
—*You have a European kisser,* he says like Edward G. Robinson.
—*I'm American, pure mongrel, half Jewish.*
—*Me too, I trace back to a mystic philosopher from Lisbon.*
—*Stop, you're making me nervous.*
—*How is Mexico treating you?*
—*At the bullfights this matador dedicated his victory to me.*
Then some jerk said the bull-fighter was an amateur.

I said, 'Maybe, but the bull's a professional.'
Close on the tip of her tongue between her teeth as she untwists wires.
He settles Paulette down on pillows.
She looks, from that height, at his zipper:—*Now what?*
—*Now we wait for the magic…*
Did you know I was raised by a bruja?
You see, my twin Carlito died before we were one.
My mother fell upon his grave, wouldn't leave the cemetery.
My father sent me to Antonia while he struggled for my mother's sanity.
—*So you have two mothers, and one is a witch?*
— *A curendera who helps the poor miners at the Valenciana.*
When I arrived I didn't have much will to live…
—*Understandable, your birth mother was…grieving…*
—*I was 'off my feed,' but Antonia had a plan.*
She convinced a she-goat to be my third mother.
I suckled at her udders and became the man you see.
Paulette looks up at him, dumbstruck, awestruck.
I'm more animal than man, he laughs.
She gets up to give him a kiss, but he pulls back.
She pouts:—*Don't you like me?*
—*It's hard for a man, one of whose mothers was a goat,*
to take himself seriously.
—*You and Frida are getting a divorce, right?*
—*Alas*, he sighs.
As Diego leans for the comfort of her kiss
Frida's pet spider monkey, Fulang, jumps on her shoulder,
its tail long and thick as a black snake. Paulette shrieks.
Diego carries him over the bridge to Frida's half of the house, returns.
—*I've had rivals in love, but that…*
Diego takes Paulette in his arms:—*You move me,*
like the inherent beauty of…
—*Aw, shucks, Diego…*
She looks for something to change the subject to.
She points to a charcoal on the wall:—*What about that?*
A pig-nosed general dancing with donkey-head politician

each picking the other's pocket…
Where are you, in the picture?
Diego points to a grinning skull labeled *Eternidad.*
He slaps his forehead:—*O God! I'm to meet Trotsky!*
—*The Trotsky? When?*
—*Five. Is it five?*
—*I'll tell you a secret that works with cars…*
You hit the gas, never the brakes, you hold your breath,
and you get there, on time…
As he heads to the door, Paulette calls out:—*Hey!*
He comes back, snatches her up in his arms.
She reaches down to the bulge in his pants…
O my, she murmurs in his ear.

A Dream and a Waking

Seaward winds, white-caps, scales on bay waters
dissolve to beaten pewter plates on an oaken dinner table
in a Ukrainian farm house where a bearded man
in Persian-wool hat like a tilted crown
cuts into a boiled potato, speaks without looking up:
—*You organized my peasants against me,*
     I had to have you arrested.
—*We must help the wretchèd of the earth, Father.*
The salt-and-pepper man stabs air with two-pronged fork:
—*But you're not wretchèd! I've worked hard to give you*
     all the advantages…
—*And the revolution will reward your sacrifices…*
—*Revolution! God!*
—*God has nothing to do with it…*
—*God hears the fall of a sparrow!*
Out the window, a young woman beside a garden fence
with a little boy: —*O, look, Lyova! a jewel box!*
She bends to pick it up; it turns into a hissing viper
     uncoiling, slithering away.
—*I will bring this cruel aristocracy down.*
His father pounds the table: —*We must look out for ourselves!*
Lyova, kneel now, ask forgiveness before Adonai.
—*Shall I grovel in darkness even as I fear and hate my neighbors?*
—*Are you no longer a Jew?*
—*I am beyond tribalism. The revolution will sweep away the past…*
—*A Jew is a Jew and the pogrom will always come back.*
The father's eyes well up:
—*I fear the time has come for you to leave my house…*
Out the window a woman in white furs walks a snowy hill.
—*It is not your house, it is my mother's house!*

Close Iris   **Open Iris**

As church bells toll Leon's eyelids blink open
from the dream of his first exile. He rises, looks
in the dresser mirror, draws his eyelids down
to check for bloodshot, pours water from pitcher
to basin, takes his pajama top off, bares his
chalk white skin, looks out a window where
a steaming January splashes morning from broken
drainpipes, rising fog shimmers orange tile roofs,
a parrot shrieking in the garden's bamboo thickets—
lizards cling to stucco walls with acid claws.
He turns to a photograph of Lenin in
Persian-wool hat:—*What Sheol is this, Vladamir*
Illych, where it never snows? I received your law
but the False Prophet built the Golden Distraction.
I tried to call the people back to the true path,
but Stalin had already begun the orgy.
He picks up a glass ball with a dacha at its center,
shakes it. Clear liquid alive with snowflake swirls.
He turns the photograph of Lenin to the wall:
No time now for regrets… he snarls, baring his teeth.
I have been ruthless, I can be ruthless, I will be ruthless!
His face softens, can not hold its grimace.
He shakes a fist at his image in the mirror.

An Assassin Is Born

A young man in white tropical suit blends
almost invisibly into a hotel suite in Empire décor.
Red roses in an amphora on the gold-trimmed fireplace mantle,
a Soviet flag draped on the glass-topped sofa table.
A slim, middle-aged woman in black sheath,
high-heels, pearls, holds a photo album open:
—*Look, Ramon, it's you, the golden boy at summer camp.*
A photo of four sun-bleached boys smiling arm-in-arm.
To one side, a pale scout with downcast eyes.
—*We never had any fun, it was a bootcamp for little revolutionaries.*
—*Fun? In a world so full of suffering?*
In the gilded mantle mirror, Ramon
with the slicked-back look of a European lady-killer.
—*You could go to Hollywood and be the next Valentino.*
—*Honestly, mother.* He smooths his hair.
—*Do this for humanity*
—*It's not for humanity, it's for him.*
Ramon juts his chin at a man stirring martinis at a dry bar.
—*It's for Stalin,* the double-breasted suit says,
carrying three cocktails on a tray.
Isn't this the style?
All three drink greedily, without ceremony.
The older man flashes a photo: a blond, with Modigliani nose.
Her name is Sylvia Agelof, Trotsky's personal secretary.
Ramon looks, winces. His mother leers:
—*Just close your eyes, Ramon, get your hands on her body.*
—*What do you want me to do, Isaak?*
—*Go to Paris.* Isaak pulls papers from his coat pocket.
You'll be Jacques Mornard, a Belgian businessman. Try it.
—*'Bonjour, je m'appelle Jacques.'*
The woman reaches behind his head,

pulls him toward her, his forehead touching hers:
— *She's vain, Ramon, as only a half-beautiful woman can be*
    When you fall for her, she'll believe it.
Isaak sneers:—*A playboy, you can do that, can't you?*
The woman shakes the Soviet flag in Isaak's face:
—*We need him! Don't be snide.*
Isaac flinches:—*Yes, Caridad.*
—*What then?* the new Jacques lights a victory cigarette.
—*She'll lead you right into the old man's house.*
Caridad curls the hair at the back of Ramon's neck:
—*He's a madman who won't rest until Stalin is dead.*
It's all vendetta with him, just like your father.
Isaak puts a record on the victrola:
    There may be troub-le a-head
    But while there's moonlight
    and mu-sic and and ro-mance,
    let's face the mu-sic and dance...
Isaak clasps Ramon's mother to him in a quick foxtrot.
—*Your mother is with us, Ramon. Just don't think about it.*
—*How can I not? To kill a man?*
Caridad dances as if assaulting Franco's barricades.
Ramon's hand floats up with its own life
to touch her shoulder. Louvered blinds stripe
over Ramon's body. He stares down at a white-faced
mime on the sidewalk below. He points his finger,
cocks his thumb. His hand jerks back as he
shoots the street performer, who falls
to the soundless laughter of a crowd.
Freeze frame.

Diego Shows Leon the House

Here's the kitchen, right off the terrace
with yellow tile walls just like the house
in Guanajuato where I learned the most
important thing for me is to make art.
And what you want the most in life is
to save the Soviet Union from Stalin.

Every day I wake in your strange land
where it never snows and go to work
writing articles to show the world
the monster that he is, but then I
reach out to touch a flower, and I'm
troubled by a new "as if," for it seems
as if in the long view, it doesn't matter
whether Stalin lives or dies or signs
a non-aggression pact with Hitler,
insane as that sounds...

Fine, I'll sketch you waving triumphant
at May Day paraders from the Kremlin
balcony...Look, an electric ice-box, the
latest thing...

...I'm plagued by visions that after the
war, after Europe lies in ruins, life will
go on, but humankind can no longer
trust itself, the family tree poisoned,
and men will invent mehcanisms to
carry out their tyrannies so they can
wash their hands of the blood, and
skies will turn a prison gray...

15

Antonia taught me in Guanajuato to believe
that everything alive owes everything to
the dead, who are with us but not visible,
as gods buried in cornfields are not visible
but real...

>...and if men imagine their enemy's
ranks filled with dead souls then they'll
match them death for death, until
there's nothing but the self-mockery
of those who have wasted their lives
in make-believe, nauseous with worry
they'll find their hollowness out, and
find themselves wishing the anxious
acting would be over...

...and when time came for me to go to
the capitol to learn to make the invisible
manifest, Antonia conjured the spirit of the
well who showed us where the silver was
so I could stand beside Posada and learn
art's symphony of color, its gyratory volumes,
its realized forms that trigger illumination!
And when I left Mexico to learn from Picasso
how to break everything apart so the black
light of this sad century shone out, I woke,
shanghaied on a ship, my pockets full of gold
from Diaz's general, my rival for the love of
a beautiful actress...

>...and I could say, *"Apres moi, l'deluge,"*
except it gives me no joy, so I instead
say I now believe in a future where we
will all repossess our lives.

...and when I sailed home, Antonia knew
and walked six days to greet me, screaming
at my birth mother, "I am his soul! What are
you?" and they throttled each other until they
wept and knew they were sisters. Frida has
known this from the start—there are many
women—ones to give birth, ones to give
dreams. *Mira!* I've sketched you Stalin's death
mask, never mind your objection it's not real.
I find it more useful to believe everything.

Dream of an Afternoon

Leon unlocks the studio and as it
swings open, sunbeams from skylights.
Close on dust in slow-motion swirls, puffs
at each footfall. Cut to a print by Posada
pinned to a wall. In the sky, a comet-man
dives, all teeth, toward men, women,
scattering, arms up, imploring heaven.
Church towers topple, some are flung
off the earth... he sees soldiers pulling
a Nicholas II statue down with ropes.
He turns to Diego's self-portrait, the artist
as a boy surrounded by his national ghosts,
a frog peeping from his pocket, he,
holding the hand of "La Caterina," skeleton
woman, skull festooned with ostrich plumes,
bones draped with feather boa...Leon
smiles at Diego's humor: her feather boa
is a skeleton of a boa constrictor. His eyes
focus on Frida holding a Taoist cue-ball,
staring out to a future Leon imagines as
him, he, waltzing her into the air above
bronze-green fountains, Aztec chiefs,
Conquistadores, statues of dead heroes...
Benito Juarez...Hidalgo in priestly collar...
Morelos' bandana-covered head... Madero
murdered, Zapata murdered, Carranza,
Huerta exiled, a bloodless death. The
fingertips of both Leon's hands skim,
as if guided by a ouiji board planchett,
across Frida's painted lips,
envying the sunlight that touches them.

Pyramid of the Sun

A large sand cone. Red ants climb up,
down, a swarm comes bearing a bright green
preying mantis, fighting, cutting its tormentors in half
with enormous claws. Natalia, Frida, Leon, Diego
    dots half-way up the temple steps.
Leon heaves himself up, wills himself up.
When Frida stops, he stops, presses hand to heart.
—*Are you all right?*
—*I'm overwhelmed. Think of the ceaseless, heart-breaking labor…*
—*If I can do it, you can do it.*
—*No, I…you don't…* She starts climbing again.
He reaches out to grasp her hand, but she is three steps up.
At the top, they flock, look down. Below,
color-streams of visitors *blur* on the Avenue of the Dead.
Diego points to stone statues, tilted back, faces
staring into the sun:—*Sometimes I hear their voices.*
One says, 'Since time began, it must end.' Another says,
'The exchange of blood is to forestall that end.'
Leon's frame wavers, looking, vertiginous, down steep steps:
—*I feel what they must've felt-awe, and terror.*
Diego raises his arms: —*Here the priests evoked the gods.*
—*What gods?* Natalia sneers with the blasé of a tired
Parisian cab-driver. Diego looks down
sees a crowd of Teotihuacános in bright costumes
who stand watching priests on platforms,
smoke rising from burnt offerings.
Leon asks Frida:—*What became of these people?*
—*They invented the straight line, then vanished into the curve.*
Leon asks Diego:—*Could you make a sculpture of me?*
Diego frames Leon with his thumbs,

visualizes him in pharaoh's costume, headdress,
        crook and flail in his crossed hands:
—*I see you as the Sphinx.*
Leon smiles:—*I am a riddle.*
Frida leans into him,
he suns himself in her gaze,
her warmth melting his Ukrainian ice.
A bi-plane carves a white scar through sky...
ESSO on its fuselage. Diego:—*Our new god.*
He sees Quetzacoatl, in feathered headdress, on a flying serpent
Leon stares at Frida as she turns, balletic, a breeze
riffling her hair, her breasts rising
as she raises her arms to embrace the valley.
Below, ants dismember the preying mantis,
separate its claws, suddenly things,
and drag its head into the hole.

Diego Drives Leon to Cuernavaca

South over pine green mountains
to the Palace of Cortés to show Leon and his bodyguard
Jesús the murals he painted when Frida and he were
just married and she was still on fire
with the holy mission of bearing him a son,
whom she said would be a god.
They climb a tall staircase. Leon stops, out-of-breath.
—*Cortés built his palace on the ruins of an Aztec temple,*
hence the many steps, Diego explains.
—*Typical imperialist trick,* Leon winks.
At the top, a mural leans over them:
Conquistadors roll a calendrical stone off a cliff
to smash the Aztec's belief in the solidity of time.
Leon's eyes follow a trail of smashed underbrush
to the gorge's bottom. The stone has withstood the fall.
Cortés and two Aztec chiefs in white plumes
stand beside it: An astonished look on Cortés' face.
Next panel—an Aztec warrior in jaguar skins
plunges his stone dagger into a Spaniard's throat.
Leon nods:—*You know war.*
Diego says: —*When the revolution broke out*
I was an itinerant artist who carried dynamite fuses in my paintbox.
I would arrive in a town and Boom! trainloads of Diaz's
        mercenaries would crash into a gorge.
In an arched doorway, a man hunched under a black fedora.
In next mural: Spaniards prod natives with ten-foot pikes.
One native crawls under the lash, half iguana, half man.
Leon sees cigarette smoke billow
past a mural of Zapata standing beside a white horse.
The mural comes alive: a campesino steps toward Zapata,

fires a pistol. *All I know,* Diego says, *is white smoke*
goes to white horse. Leon turns to Jesús, finger to lips,
Jesús sees the smoke, begins to stalk along the wall.
Leon [*in stage voice*]:—*Are you a defender of the church, Diego?*
—*My maiden aunt took me to the Church of San Diego*
when I was five. I ran to the altar. Idiots! I cried
to the faithful with their hands full of black beads,
there is only air and birds, not little boys with wings!
My aunt took me home and spanked me
until my little man stood up.
Leon stares at Diego:—*Have you no shame?*
—*My art requires me to abandon it.*
Jesús spins the stranger, flattens his face against a wall,
fishes a stiletto out of the man's back pocket.
—*You can't do this to me!* the man yells.
—*Did Stalin send you?*
—*Answer!* Jesús smacks the man with his own hat.
—*Take him to the Museum Director's office, call the police.*
Jesús shoves the man down the corridor. Leon
collapses on a bench, rubbing his temples:
—*Absurd distractions dog my life…*
He stares up at the Zapata mural—*What a beautiful white horse.*
—*Frida asked why I painted it white when it was black.*
I said. 'The artist should paint beautiful legends for the people.'
Leon fingers the stiletto as if it were a crucifix,
its blade pops from its handle, clattering to the stone floor.
She is acid and tender, hard as steel,
       yet delicate as butterfly wings
—*If you still love her, why the divorce?*
— *We believe if we aren't honest with our feelings our art will die.*
We love each other madly, but we keep exploding the house.
Leon puts his hands to his temples, totters to his feet.
—*What's wrong?*
Leon mutters:—*A migraine, so bad it has blinded me.*
Diego leads Leon slowly back down the stairs

to the parked station wagon. Jesús jumps
into back seat. They roar off down the street,
Leon's face against the window, his eyes like gray birds
that have seen too many bleak dawns.
—*I had my first attack the night Kerensky fell.*
Stalin spread the rumor that I was epileptic. Unfit.
Diego stops the car on a suspension bridge:
—*Can you open your eyes?*
Wire cables moor the bridge to both cliffs of a deep canyon,
wind whistles through like aeolian harps.
Leon steps out into the wind, suit coat flapping,
leans on the rail, looking down:
—*This gorge is like the one in your mural.*
—*It is the one in my mural.*
Drawing in a deep breath:
—*Someone's out there plotting to kill me, Diego,*
and all I can do is try to live each day
as an act of faith in the future.
Diego puts a painted egg in Leon's hand:
Leon looks at the egg: a ring of peasant farmers,
men and women, holding hands.
Above them the words "The earth is ours!"
Diego puts his hand on Leon's shoulder:
—*Think of this as the better world you dream of.*
        One day it will hatch out.
Mexico's spaces are boundless, Leon, her
        consolations, boundless…

Don't Make Me Laugh

Leon, Frida, in the studio of the Blue House:
he looks up at a painting of a woman lying on a brass bed,
her eyes blank xs, red mouths of wounds on her body,
her hoodlum lover leaning on a nicotine yellow wall,
pares his nails with a stiletto…
Leon points to Diego's sketch,
        puffs of white smoke from Maximillian's rifles,
           campesinos falling.
—*Yours is so different.*
She stiffens:—*Is there not a common sense of outrage?*
—*But Diego's isn't personal.*
Frida picks up a rose made from a tin can with shears,
hands it to Leon. He cups it ginterly:
—*That's the effect I was trying for.*
She plucks the red bloom from him, sets it back on a table.
Ah, let's get out of here, it smells like a mausoleum.
Frida leans on him as he helps her down the staircase.
When they reach the landing he's sweating.
and like any man with an official version of himself
he turns away to daub his face. In her bedroom,
the four-poster with its white canopy
on which a doll resembling her sleeping self is perched.
On a shelf, a terra-cotta figurine: an Aztec goddess,
gritting her teeth, giving birth.
Inside her chest, a god astride a flying serpent.
—*What is this?*
—*Coatlique, and Tezcatlipoca , he who sees*
the heart's cruelest secrets, the person inside her person.
Frida sits on the chenille bedspread. On the wall
in a star, portraits of Marx, Engels, Lenin, Mao, Stalin.

—*Why am I not among your pantheon?*
—*Look up.* A painting on the arched ceiling:
Moses holding a staff over the waters, his third eye open.
From solar, lunar discs Egyptian hands of light descend.
—*You are a flame that gives hope to the poor.*
He laughs:—*Ah, so that's how you see me.*
Leon takes a red *papier maché* goat mask from the wall.
—*Careful. He who dons the mask becomes the god.*
—*I know, and then is killed, a human sacrifice...*
—*If he who wears the mask is the god, there is no human sacrifice...*
Through the mask he sees Frida unbuttoning her blouse,
unfastening her body-cast with its painted
Corinthian column, cracked in six places.
[Super: Picasso's "Guernica," one beat, two beats, gone.]
—*It's amazing you can walk at all...*
—*Please, no pity. I'm not sick, I'm broken,*
but I'm happy to be alive, as long as I can paint.
She holds up, examines, her hands: *Can you know my longings,*
                you, who've already made history?
—*Are you going to take a siesta?*
—*Not alone.*
She places her hand behind his head,
looks into his eyes. The room gets agitated, humming,
a thousand orange monarch butterflies in the room,
opening, closing their wings. Leon chokes.
—*You can touch me.* She puts his hand on her breast..
—*You have a warmth that melts me...*
Frida loosens his tie, unbuttons his collar, peels off his coat:
What do you need from me?
Frida lies back on her pillows, softly:
—*I need a new fire, a vortex, a...*Leon kisses her throat :
—*I need someone to love me, not this name*
                I stole from a Siberian prison warden...
                With you, I could be a man like other men...
—*I hope you won't be. With Diego, making love is like*

being rolled over by the entire Gulf of Mexico...
[Leon covers a smile with his hand]
...I prayed that you would give me your ruthlessness.
Leon murmurs into her hair:—*It's not mine.*
—*Aren't you the man who signed death warrants for those boys,*
        those Naval cadets, on the Neva River?
—*Don't you know everything interesting happens*
        outside of right and wrong?
She holds the mask to her face, speaks through it:
—*Deliver me from my tormentor*
—*Diego?*
—*Me, the good little girl.*
She probes Leon's chest, seeking an opening,
        holds up a gold chain with a cameo of Lenin.
The person inside your person was never you, was it?
It was something, a force, beyond you, working through you.
He kisses the inside of her wrist: —*Is this the hand*
you paint with? Your genius, I believe in that...
—*Sponsor me as Lenin sponsored you.*
—*Yes, but, first, forgive me... On the steppes*
where I was born, we don't talk when we make love...
—*It was only your mask talking.*
—*What mask?*
—*Don't make me laugh. It only hurts when I laugh!*
She kisses, bites, his lower lip. Leon winces, his blood
stains his tongue... *How do gods make love,*
except with a wounding kiss? In every love
there's a victim, Leon... I am Diego's... Natalia is yours...
You are mine...

Meanwhile, in Paris

Through French windows, wet snow falling
through hot pink neon streaks of Parisian sunset.
Leon's son, Lev Sedov, sits at a desk, the livingroom strewn
with galley sheets, a picture of his mind as Cubist collage.
Lev reads a letter under yellow lamplight:
—*Listen to this!* he calls to Jeanne in the kitchen.
She, bent at the waist, serves a ten-year-old boy dinner.
My father's in the Coyoacán market to buy flower pots.
He and Diego haggle with this artisan.
He says, 'If I buy a dozen pots surely I should get a discount.'
'No,' says the potter, 'To make identical pots I've had to
deaden my soul. Therefore I must get my price.'
—*Ha! a new wrinkle on the labor theory!*
—*He ought to have written novels instead of fomenting revolution.*
—*You ought to write novels.*
—*Don't start. Can't I be happy for my father,*
that in Mexico he's left the dungeon phase of his life?
She steps into the doorway:—*What's he want this time?*
—*To check on airline schedules from Berlin to Oslo.*
—*Whatever for?* lights a cigarette with a kitchen match from her slacks.
—*Stalin now says my father is a terrorist.*
She leans on the doorframe: —*Is spring ever going to come?*
then puts Tchaikovsky on the phonograph, violins strike up:
Whoo-whoowhoowhoo-whoowhoo-whoowhoo
Lev's body jerks with surprise.
—*I'm going to my room now,* the boy Seva whispers.
Lev stands: —*How are your studies going?*
—*Very well, in Biology,* the boy answers.
Whee-wheewhee-wheewhee-whoowhoo-whoowhoo...
Lev embraces him:—*Make us proud...*

Seva walks to his room. Lev to Jeanne:
I'm writing a letter to the Paris newspapers.
It says if I'm found dead I was murdered by Stalin's goons...
She stubs out her cigarette: —*I don't want to love*
a martyr or a saint, Lev, just an ordinary man
        I can grow old with.
A thunder crash booms outside their windows.
Jeanne buries herself in Lev's lapels.
They stand rocking like slow dancers.
—*It's Stalin,* Lev laughs. *He makes thunder in winter.*
He infects my sister's mind with thoughts of suicide
        from a thousand miles away!
—*Please, don't talk like that...*
—*It's only the insane reality of the world we live in.*
—*I'm just not good under pressure. I'm a scaredy-cat.*
It's like having a crazy person in my family, I...
A knock on the door: Jeanne's face, a question mark
Trumpets count *one, two, three, four, five, six, seven, eight.*
At the door a middle-aged man, epaulets of snow,
the weasel-eyed look of a married man who goes with prostitutes.
—*My name is Krivitzky, I've something to tell you.*
—*Come.*
He steps into the apartment, Jeanne takes his coat.
Lev walks into the kitchen, returns with a tea service.
—*I'm in the International Section.*
You would probably call me one of Stalin's goons.
I hate the Hitler-Stalin pact, but I love my country...
—*My father faces the same dilemma.*
Trombones blare in a broad waltz, *Bah-bah-bah-bah, bah bah!*
—*That's why your father lost control.*
Everything becomes ambiguous, direct action is not possible.
Jeanne frowns, tired of the rhetoric, the political clichés.
—*Why are you here?*
—*To warn you of a traitor, I don't have a name, but...*

Another knock at the door.
Krivitsky whispers… *is there a back way out?*
Jeanne nods, leads him through the kitchen.
Krivitsky stops: *They are sending a Spaniard to kill your father.*
The final line: *One-two, three-four-five, six-six!*
Lev opens the door to a blond young man in Polish student's cap.
—*Mark! I didn't expect you so soon.*
Mark scans the room, the teapot, the three cups.
—*Sounds like you started the party without me.*
Wasn't that the Nutcracker? [wave at Jeanne]
Hello, beautiful. Jeanne smirks.
Wrapping a scarf around his neck Lev kisses Jeanne
farewell and the two men rush out the door.
Jeanne sits on the sofa alone.
She tries to put the tea cups and saucers on the serving tray,
but they clatter in her hands. She throws them
down one by one on the threadbare carpet,
then kneels to look at the shattered fragments,
reading the shards of china like runic stones.
She leans back laughing,
daubing wet eyes with her sleeves:
—*What's the matter, scaredy-cat? Why the tears?*

Labyrinth of Madness

On the sidewalk Lev, Mark, bend into wind-driven snow...
Lev clutches his stomach.
—*Are you ill?*
—*Think of it, Mark. Zinoviev's going to be executed*
Kamenev, my uncle, who used to wrestle on the floor with Sergei and me—
Buhkarin, Rakovsky, Smirnov, Muralov,
all members of the original Politburo, hand-picked by Lenin himself.
They're all going to beaten until they beg to be executed
*   for crimes they never committed.*
Over Mark's shoulder Lev sees Krivitsky emerge from an alleyway.
Mark gives Lev the look there is no defense for: admiration.
Flakes fall from black clouds above lurid neon skies.
Wind swirls snow up in helixes.
—*What was going on in your apartment, if I may ask?*
Lev stares at Mark, standing in a spot of sulphur streetlight:
—*We received intelligence from a dubious source.*
—*About what, if I may ask?*
—*The whole thing, the myth of the Opposition...*
—*The cause to which you've devoted your life is a myth?*
Lev shivers:—*I need a drink.*
—*How long have you felt this... this, what?*
—*Since Stalin had my father exiled... do you know*
the classical myth of Hercules and Antaeus? Once Stalin
lifted my father off the soil of Mother Russia
he was a dead man...
—*Why do you go on, then?*
—*Who do you mean when you say 'you'?*
—*You, the only you...*
—*No, there's the you who now believes in nothing,*
a cynic who drowns himself in alcohol and sex.

Then there's the you who goes on with his father's struggle
out of nostalgia for one wild October… Lev winces,
clutching his stomach… *when life was*
an intoxicating circus like one of those nights
in an American revival tent when all believe they are saved,
only to wake in the morning back in their lives of
intimidation and defeat by which they barter their souls
        for their daily bread…
The streetlights go out, everything pitch-black.
It's Stalin! Lev laughs. *He blacks out the City of Light!*
He slips, falls on the snow-covered sidewalk.
A floral delivery lorry rumbles around the corner,
        headlights like twin swords.
Mark jumps aside as it humps up the curbstone.
A funeral wreath falls out and lands on Lev's chest.
Lev grasps the flowers, smiling: *—Not a good sign, is it?*
He gasps. *Hospital.*
—Not a city hospital, Stalin's agents will find you!
Mark flicks his cigarette lighter on, dashes up the street,
looking for a telephone, his hand cupping the flame.

Burning the Judases

Night: the study. Leon paces, alone,
stops to gaze into the garden, where a monkey
rocks as it shakes the bars of its bamboo cage.
Distant snare-drumbeats spark like gunfire.
The telephone rings, Leon flinches, picks up the receiver.
—*Yes?* listens a moment...*Diego? plotting to murder me?*
looks at telephone at arm's length...*Who is this?*
slams the receiver down. He paces to his right,
stops before a photograph of Lenin:
—*Maybe I should confide in Diego, tell him that*
when you died, Stalin sent a cable—"Earth frozen,
funeral delayed..."then ordered the mummification,
so he delivered the eulogy, he took the leadership...
He paces to his left: *No, I should not burden Diego.*
My memory, my regret, my anger...
he takes several deep breaths, sits at his desk...
the answer is always work, work, work, writing these dispatches.
A sharp tap on his window—pane startles him.
In the glass, Fulang, the monkey, *Eternidad* on its headband
Eeeech! it cries...someone's pulled its tail.
Leon finds the monkey sitting on Diego's shoulder:
—*What are you doing out there?*
—*Playing with my monkey.*
—*You are a world-famous painter,* Leon hectors.
You must create a zone of dignified inaccessibility about your person.
Diego laughs:—*I would find it creepy to make a false space.*
Diego walks around through the doorway into study:
Come to the burning of the Judases.
Leon holds up a newspaper to Diego with its big headline:
TROTSKY'S PLAN TO KILL STALIN
TROTSKY UNMASKED AS HILTLER AGENT

—The lies I have daily to contend with.
I can feel Stalin's goons out there. It's not me alone
he wants to kill, it's the human imagination.
—Certainly you will escape him, Leon.
He turns to face Diego: *—So far…so far…*
You have the land you know so well, while to me it is this…jungle.
—Maybe this 'jungle' can serve you Let me be your guide.
— Too little time…
—Don't you trust me?
—Ah, you just love melodrama…
he points to the photograph of him and Lenin
> *What do you see?*
Diego shrugs:*—You were friends.*
—Perhaps I placed Lenin inside my chest…
—Ah, the person inside your person…
—…as if he were something I could be true to.
But that is wrong, I have my mission…to rescue the revolution…
Fulang starts to pull books off shelves.
Can't you control your monkey?
—Never! Diego laughs.
Leon collapses, also laughing, in his chair.
Diego stares at Leon's silence:*—So, you are grieving…*
—If I'm silenced, no one will ever know what might have been…
—Forgive my intrusion, then…
—No, I want to come out with you now. I have to trust someone,
> *or what's left of my life won't be worth living.*
Diego slings Fulang on his shoulder:
—Good! there's someone I want you to meet.

The Writing on the Wall

A street festival dances around Diego, Leon.
Men bear aloft on white crosses, a *papier maché* Bandit Hero
in big sombrero wielding his sword, leering priest
figures, bumping their heads against stars.
Drums, trumpets, shouts, torches:
—*I can see why you paint crowd scenes!*
—*My paintings are poetry for the illiterate!*
They weave down Allende toward the zócalo, past electric lights
strung from tree to tree as rockets shoot phosphorescent
hisses, men set off bonfires. The Judas-figures
go up in flames that reflect off colonial church walls,
pink, orange, green. Leon's eyes follow
a swirling trail of sparks, bell towers seem to tilt,
men on their knees raise their arms
dressed out like cactus limbs, beseeching Heaven.
—*It's like Posada's "End of the World."*
—*Ah, here we are!* Diego pulls Leon down a little lane,
jiggles the doorbell. An elderly man in
tuxedo, red slippers, holding a skeleton mask:
—*Ah, Diego! And who is this?*
He inspects Leon through his pince-nez.
—*Don Rosario, show my friend Leon your flea circus.*
—*I'm preparing for a night on the town, but come.*
The skeleton mask conducts them through the corridor
to a greenhouse in the back yard. Don Rosario
throws a switch: Spread out before them
a model of a European city-churches, parks with lawns.
—*Here come the fleas!*
—*Where?* Leon squints, begins to scratch his neck.
—*Marching, like the shadow of a cloud over the streets.*
Behind him Leon hears the words:

The more one believes, the more one sees
In the fairy-tale city of the King of the Fleas.
Leon sees a building like the St. Petersburg Winter Palace:
—*The revolution,* he whispers.
—*These are no ordinary fleas, they aspire to freedom and dignity.*
Leon mutters to Diego:—*You can't do this to me,*
    I'm a hero of the Revolution.
—*Everyone has his Judas, Leon.*
—*No arguing, caballeros, it disturbs the fleas.*
Don Rosario flips the light off, the greenhouse goes dark,
the greenhouse door swings open,
muffled drums again.
Outside Don Rosario's house Diego takes Leon by the elbow:
—*I'll walk you back.*
Leon yanks his arm away.
The Judases go up in flames. Leon's shadow,
silhouetted by bonfires cast against a wall, spark
bursts light graffiti:
    Crush the Trotskyite Vermin!
—*The sky is full of disaster tonight,* Diego says,
leading him back to the gates of the Blue House.
Pink rockets light Leon's sweat-stung eyes:
—*Get me a dozen white rabbits I can care for, Diego.*
In a rain of sparkles Leon sees more graffiti:
    Jesús has died, Marx has died,
    and I don't feel so good either.
He leans against the wall as if he could not stand
without it, bent double from laughing, his hand
beside a cartoon of himself where his forehead
is circled by a crown of thorns made of bayonets.

Frida Renders the Mock Trial

The Blue House, its *galleria* walls cross-hatched
with noontime window mullion shadows.
Frida, a sketchbook in her lap,
Fulang on Diego's shoulder, nibbles a banana,
chattering like the international press corps on folding chairs.
The judges enter in dark business suits, ties.
In Frida's pastel crayon drawing
they wear iridescent parrot feather cloaks,
gold bangles on naked ankles, chests draped
with the green stones the gods loved.
On their heads wooden effigies of eagles,
jade eyes above yellow beaks:—*All rise!*
In Frida's sketch John Dewey is an Aztec eagle priest
with thick spectacles banging his gavel,
in Frida's picture a stone war-club.
Police snap to attention,
machine guns slung from shoulders.
Natalia stands with the aid of Sylvia Agelof.
—*Begin the proceedings! Bring in the accused!*
Leon and his lawyer walk into the room,
stand before the plumed tribunal.
Frida draws his thumbs tied behind his back,
a bubble where words hang above Dewey's head
in a retablo:—*It is a matter of utmost concern
to human conscience that no man be condemned
without due process. While this gathering
does not have the force of law it will conduct itself
according to the highest ideals of jurisprudence.*
The bailiff ascends a rostrum of human skulls,
stone tablet in his hands:—*The charges:*

Conspiracy to commit sabotage, terror, assassination.
—*Insane!* Natalia cries from her chair.
Boom! goes Dewey's gavel:—*No outbursts!*
Nothing will be permitted to lessen the dignity of this court.
Leon:—*Will I not be permitted to challenge the charges?*
—*Mr. Goldman, advise your client that I will maintain order.*
These proceedings will not degenerate into a circus.
Leon continues:—*But either the record of history,*
secret letters from Lenin naming me heir to Party leadership
which I offer from personal archives
       or Stalin lies, to silence my opposition…
—*The accused may make no personal attacks;*
       he will receive an impartial trial.
Laughter erupts among the press corps.
Frida makes Leon's heart visible as flames
reaching up into his brain like tendrils.
Goldman leans to Leon, conferring inaudibly:
—*May it please the court, my client wishes*
to raise a point of logic. He asks, 'If I have so many
co-conspirators, why am I not the Soviet?'
—*I don't want arguments, I want proof.*
—*My client's proofs are notorized travel receipts*
which I now place in evidence… he rises, waving
a sheaf of papers…*Stalin charges my client*
conspired in Oslo when he was obviously elsewhere.
These schedules prove there were no flights
from Berlin to Oslo on the day in question.
What else in Stalin's charges is fabricated?
This is no 'show trial' where Stalin can torture his
       victims into false self-incrimmiations.
Leon rises, holding the painted egg Diego gave him:
—*Once, the people of a poor backward country*
rose up against a cruel aristocracy. That example
still stands as humanity's greatest hope.

Since I have been in Mexico I have learned its principle
from a parable my friend Diego Rivera has told me.
It is said that when men were first created
all they had was a spoon six feet long to eat with,
and they would have starved to death as they could
find no way to bring it to their lips by holding
the long end, except they learned to feed each other.
Frida whispers to Diego:—*This is Trotsky*
at his best, but his eloquence won't save him.
In her sketch Marx leans from a cloud holding
a scroll of *The Manifesto* like a thunderbolt.
Leon presses on:—*Now the people must choose*
between Hitler and Stalin, and they chose Stalin
and that is right. But in days to come, with Nazism
defeated, the people will cast off Stalin and the lie
that we have accomplished Paradise in our time,
that mankind has nothing more to hope or
struggle for. Thus, I do not despair. My life has
forged in me an indestructible temper. I hold
fast to my faith in the restlessness of the human soul,
which impels us all toward permanent revolution,
until the withering away of all states.
Leon slumps in his chair, Dewey gavels:
—*This day's proceedings are at an end.*
Frida draws the judges filing out,
their trains of parrot feathers flowing behind.
In her final sketch, Frida shows the reporters as
a flock of bats flapping out to file their stories.

Leon's Love Letter to Frida

From above, Leon on the terrace, afternoon; he is
writing in a leather-bound journal, a pen, an inkwell.
Close on his hand as he writes; birdsong in the trees.

Perhaps it is Mexico, perhaps the heat that invades my
brain as the shimmering air invades the earth through
the walls of your Blue House where I am writing this
letter as I watch the green stillness of the garden and
where I live like a man obsessed with the belief that
you could restore me. When I saw you against the sky
atop the Sun Temple in the City of the Gods I glimpsed
your divinity. I know it's no way to woo a woman to
speak of loving another years ago, yet no woman since
Alexandra Lyvovna has stirred my heart with such
tender passion. We were young revolutionaries exiled
to Ust-Kut, living in a hut between the forest and the
Lena River. At night when we looked at one another
with love eyes first we had to shut out the screams of
drunks from the saloon next door, then pinch the light
from our candle to lie in the dark, bedeviled by
cockroaches crawling over our naked bodies alone
in the vast Siberian winter.

Together we made two little girls—one who
coughed her life out years ago, one who took her life it
seems only yesterday rather than face Stalin's dungeons—
and we stayed sane because we were young and read
Marx to each other during those fifty below zero nights
and because we dreamed of escape to London to join
Lenin, to write for the Bolshevik newspaper, Iskra, which
means "the spark" in English, the language I must use
here. She sent me away when my chance came "You

must," she whispered as we held each other one last time.
Yet I remember her eyes with such regret. I don't
want to make that mistake again, Frida.

Jean van Heijenoort walks out onto the terrace
carrying a sheaf of papers:—Sorry to bother you,
but these require your signature immediately, sir.
Leon fights an initial annoyance at being interrupted:
—Not now, my dear boy, not now. [smiles]
Can't you see I'm in the throes of inspiration?
—Perhaps later, then, Jean says as he withdraws.
Leon dips his pen in the inkwell, resumes writing:
        My marriage to Natalia is… how shall I say?
We have nothing left between us but our sons. Not a
word passes. In public she pushes me to keep the faith
with "the Opposition." How crazy I must
sound, weighing a life of struggle against the slim
chance of finding happiness with you. Don't think I
haven't heard you say, "I tire of el viejo," I have enough
Spanish for that It's the truth. I am sixty years old,
and you but half my age. I know it's not wise to speak
of one's empty marriage. It's so bourgeois I shake with
shame. If you reject me again I will tell myself that as
I love you I should leave you alone. People close to me
turn up dead.
        Yet I find myself sitting here, melting in this
August afternoon in the invisible ink of my sweat, writing
words utterly alien to me, words about your lush garden
as the future I once imagined. Before me lies the bright
green strip of grass beneath your wall, the clear blue
sky above, and sunlight everywhere. Life is beautiful.
Let the next generation cleanse it of evil. I feel as if I
have died already, already given my life to my ideals,
and the fires of my October have spent themselves in ash.

Yet with the last ember of my soul I dream of you and
me on the coast near Tehuantepec, you painting, I writing,
both of us at last finding the peace we need to create.
Am I mad? If so, I go on embracing this dream of
embracing you until death and the tides shall cease.

The Manifesto

Diego Rivera, André Breton stroll in the gardens.
Fulang sits on Diego's shoulder, chattering seriously
as if about André's belief in chance as the last appeal.
— *Diego, tell Leon his writing is his gift to humanity.*
I feel his appeal in my spirit side, his call to
permanent revolution is to permanent revelation,
he heaps in my heart the everlasting crusade against
contentment, as a poet might, who refuses to fall asleep
      in the arms of his last good metaphor...
Against the wall, Leon washes out a rabbit hutch,
baby-talking his white friends as they hop among flowers:
—*You would acquit me, wouldn't you, my friends?*
Leon joins the two men as they walk into the *galleria*,
stands before one of Diego's paintings:
      A foggy night, sulphur-colored streetlight
      on the Wall Street sign and below, in subway vaults
      rows of corpses under white sheets.
—*What is the title, Diego?* André asks.
—*'Cold Storage.' The capitalists who jumped from Wall Street*
skycrapers have had themselves frozen. They will be back.
—*Why did you leave the Communist party?*
—*The absurd demand that artists leave their work to man the barricades.*
Leon picks up notepad, pencil:—*We should begin our manifesto.*
Breton urges: —*Begin with an image:*
the obscene spectacle of Nuremberg mobs burning books.
—*Demand complete freedom of artistic expression,* Diego adds.
Did you know that Hitler is a failed art student?
Frida walks in, dressed in denim: —*Gentlemen! Tea!*
Leon with the look of a man pleading backs Frida into a kitchen corner,
trying to give her something, a letter folded into a book
that falls to the floor. Natalia picks it up, reads aloud:
      When I saw you against the sky climbing

the Sun Temple… I glimpsed your divinity…
Diego sees Natalia's eyes go blank; she let s the letter
drop from her hands. Frida asks Diego:—*Got a match?*
Breton sees Frida's painting on the kitchen wall:
    a European Frida in white high-necked lace dress
    connected to a Mexican Frida by surgical tubes,
    blood splotches on both dresses.
The French poet falls on his knees, kissing Frida's feet:
—*Your painting is like a bomb wrapped in ribbons.*
This is what surrealism's meant to be, pure and cruel.
—*What's going on here?* Natalia asks. *This is most unseemly.*
André, have you gone mad? Get up off the floor.
André begs Frida:—*Let me arrange an exhibition in Paris.*
A beaming Diego gives Frida a congratulatory embrace.
—*I'll get to work right away!* She hobbles upstairs to the studio.
Breton picks himself up from floor, dusting off.
Jesús appears at the door with a little man
in Hitler moustache, bowler hat
a nervous Charlie Chaplin without a bamboo cane:
—*This man says he has a gift for you.*
Leon notices a bead of sweat running down the man's jaw,
jagged and long as an electric whine of cicadas.
Leon looks at the man as if he were a green slug.
—*L-like you, I am exiled from my native land…*
—*No, you're not…*
Boom! glass splinters fly through the room.
The little man bolts out the door through the garden.
Breton sees blood above Leon's eye:
—*You're injured!*
Leon touches his wound, inspects his bloody fingertips,
licks them off, smiling, his face aglow:
—*It's nothing, I've had entire locomotives blown up under me.*
Did you know I am the father of the Red Army?
Natalia rushes to Leon's side, crunching broken glass.
Frida bursts in, sees Leon's wound:—*Oh!*

Diego gives Leon his back—pocket bandana to wipe the blood:
—*The little man cared more for his life than his mission.*
Breton adds:—*He didn't trust his luck.*
Leon's eyes gleam: as he sits in a chair, the women kneel beside him.
He slips one arm around Frida's waist.
Natalia presses the handkerchief onto Leon's brow.
Diego sees them as a Flemish pieta that *blurs* its focus…
until only a Δ is left .

A Night on the Town

In "The Cockatoo" the swing orchestra gleams, a forest of brass,
their lapels reflect sparkles from a spinning ballroom mirror.
The bandleader conducts with his clarinet.
Sylvia and Ramon/Jacques/Frank sit at a second-row table.
—*Dance with me, Jacques, she begs.*
—*Damn it! You're supposed to call me Frank in Mexico.*
The crooner steps up to the microphone:
> *In olden days a glimpse of stocking*
> *was looked on as something shocking*
> *Now heavens knows, anything goes*
Half the trombonists swing the barrels of their horns sideways,
half bend at the waist to just miss being hit.
Dancers spin in flecks of light, a slow-spinning galaxy:
> *Good authors who once knew better words*
> *Now only use four-letter words*
> *Now heavens knows, anything goes*
Frank watches Leon at his table with Diego, Frida, Natalia,
Paulette.
Leon and Frida walk to the dance floor, she
in polished obsidian tuxedo, skips without a limp.
Frank sees the mannish Frida drives Leon so wild
he's chewing his moustache and gets up
walks out on the dance floor, cuts in, Diego
drags himself back to the table where Paulette
soothes him by rubbing his back and shoulders.
—*Come on!* Sylvia pulls Frank up out of his seat.
> *The world's gone mad today*
> *and good's bad today,*
> *and most guys today*
> *that women prize today*
> *are just silly gig-a-los...*

—*It's the Old Man's night to howl,* Sylvia laughs.

Frank sneers:—*They're all fossils, relics of the previous century.*

He dances Sylvia toward Leon, close enough to slash
his throat.—*I'm under your spell,* Frank hears Leon say.

Frida puts her hand on his chest, pushes him away:

—*It's over, whatever there was.*

Frida leaves Leon standing alone on dance floor
as the Cole Porter tune dies, applause, goes to Paulette,
holds out her hand. The songbird steps to the microphone:

> *Sometimes I wonder why I spend*
> *the lonely night, dreaming of a song...*

Frida presses Paulette to her tuxedo: Paulette says:—*You're so strong.*

—*I'm relentless,* Frida licks Paulette's ear lobe.

Paulette pulls away:—*What do you think I am, double-gaited?*

> *A melody haunts my reverie*
> *and I am once again with you...*

Leon's mouth drops open as he watched Frida try to kiss Paulette.

> *... when our love was new*
> *and each kiss an inspiration...*

Diego smiles as he watches Leon watching Frida.

Frida pulls Paulette into a dip:

—*Aren't you tired of playing the touristita?*

—*Wherever I go, doors open for me...*

Frida clasps Paulette tighter:—*I'll open your door...*

> *A nightingale sings his fairy-tale...*

Leon taps Paulette's shoulder, trying to cut in again:

—*Do you mind?*

—*Yes, I mind.*

Leon pleads: —*Give me a chance to...*

Frida waltzes away. Leon stands there, shoulders slumped.

—*What are we looking at?* Frank asks Sylvia, *heartbreak?*

—*None of our business.*

The dancers revolve in orbits around the glittering floor.
Flecks of light cross and dissolve them into atoms.
It is dancing and it isn't about
getting somewhere...and it goes on.

Ramon Dreams the Conquest

The valley spreads, an immense
lake glimmered by full moonlight.
The eye lifts to distant hills where an eagle
in a lone cactus rips a serpents' flesh.
To the south, hunched mountains,
sky pin-pricked by morning stars
burning the four points of the true Cross
        like campfires of a vast army.
Nose-flute music floats across waters.
Men carrying torches light canal waters,
not angels, though they seem to fly,
their feet invisible between thatched roof
houses on mud squares. Ramon rides
in curved steel helm across a causeway
on a bone-weary horse, slack hipped,
shambling, a heifer behind him on rope,
her cowbell clank the parody of a call
        to Holy Communion.
Loinclothed men in clusters, too
astonished to speak to these man-animals,
these centaurs. What language do
gods speak? His horse rears, spooked
by eviscerated bodies lying at a temple base.
In black sheath and pearls, his mother struggles,
her arms held by feathered warriors.
Ramon offers them the cow for his mother.
She spits vanilla beans into his outstretched hand.
Ramon, astride his horse, looks at the seeds
in his palm, puzzled by their star codex:

—Stick it in the earth! she shouts.
He dismounts, planting the seeds with his silver dagger.
First, a rumbling…then comes a beanstalk curling,
climbing fast into sky, spreading limbs,
leaves broad and thick as quarried flagstone.
He clambers up. rocking back and forth
until his green vehicle deposits him
on the temple mount
        two chapels, one red, one blue.
A boy bent over a stone altar by warriors:
—Hold him down! a priest screams,
his parrot—plumage cloak stiff with dried blood
crawling with flies, maggots.
The warriors rip open the victim's shirt,
the priest plunges an obsidian knife into his chest,
rips out his still-beating heart, drops it in flames
rising from the belly of a reclining god.
A sluggish river of smoke, blood gutters swollen,
the boy's body flung down:*—Quick! Another!*
Ramon sees the priest's blood-caked jaguar eyes
        through slits in his gold mask.
How long? Days, nights, weeks, months of slaughter
rocking like a galleon across Atlantic seas.
Ramon chokes from the stench of burning blood
as warriors wrestle another young man onto the stone.
—This has to be stopped! he cries
as he swings his sword, decapitating the priest,
whose gold mask clatters to the floor, face
revealed… the white moustache, goatee,
gleaming in pink morning light.

Calavera

Coyoacán twilight, bruise blue sky.
Leon in and out of visible, paces among bamboo
brakes, azaleas, flaming Birds of Paradise.
Aztec statues lean against adobe walls,
beyond them, exploding bottle rockets...
flak attacking bomber squadrons
in waning light sky, painted swastikas on their fuselages,
long strings of 200 pounders whistle down,
city blocks collapsing, slow-motion, onto rubbled streets,
        and in an office in the Reichstag
beneath a gilded eagle a general laughingly jokes:
—*What if the real outcome of the Spanish War*
        is to give the Kremlin to Trotsky?
Hitler bolts from his chair, stamping his foot:
—*That is not amusing, general!*
The Soviets, under the leadership of a man of real ability?
Leon nearly bumps into Diego's chest.
In his right hand, the painter holds a square box,
pulls out a human skull made of white sugar,
the word STALIN formed from clove buds
stuck in its forehead like thumb-tacks.
Diego smiles: —*This is the Mexican way of death, Leon,*
to merrily, defiantly, devour the Great Devourer.
Go ahead, put your fingers in his eye-sockets, take a bite.
Leon's hand reaches out, but he cannot touch it
Stalin's skeleton head talks, flopping its sugar bone jaw:
—*Some—thing's wrong with Trot-sky's head.*
        Let us make him dead, dead, dead!
Leon slaps the skull out of Diego's hands.
It shatters on the flagstone.

Lev Sedov's Last Hour

He awakens in a moonlit hospital room,
peels back the gauze on his abdomen. His stitches,
a row of black dragonflies sprinkled with granulated sugar.
Sand dunes clog his throat. He tilts a water carafe to his lips…
empty. He rings. Only tomb echoes.
He steadies himself on another man's bed.
—*Monpere!* the man cries out of his family dream.
Flats, planes of moonlight slant on checkerboard tiles.
The geometry of earth meets the light of heaven
to shear off his feet. Sweat pours off his forehead.
—*What is this place? Have I already died?*
Steam rises off his chest. Through its haze
Lev sees a desert of snow, pock-marked with craters,
that becomes the acned face of Josef Stalin.
The carafe slips from his hands, clangs on the floor
like a bell that speaks only one word. Surely
this angelus will bring the chanting Acolytes of Water,
bearing melted snow. All his life he has dreamed of flying,
joyless, exhausting himself, flapping his arms
just to keep from falling. Where is Jeanne, her pouting lips?
He sees himself reflected in windows, a naked frothing lunatic:
—*I should never have been born,* he says aloud.
God is the back maw of night whose glinting teeth are the stars.
He stumbles through the ward to a nurse's station
to escape being eaten. No one is guarding
the Maginot Line between the sick and the well.
He slides between wall and counter,
enters a mirrored room, sees his father, who shouts at him:
—*Will you be happy when Stalin has murdered me?*
From Lev's mouth, a strangled cry:—*Help!*

I am Lyova Sedov, son of the great revolutionary, help!
A nursing nun at last in snow-white dimple sees him
collapse, runs to him, kneels at his pulse, his lips
salivating white foam, his skin, sweaty, cold.

A Day in the Country

Leon canters across a stubble cornfield.
Mounted men in U.S. cavalry uniforms follow,
their sidearm holsters flopping on their hips.
Below them, a huge lake, ringed by mountains:
—*I'll race you!* Leon shouts, spurring his horse.
The racers leap stone walls, pass campesinos
gleaning dry corn-rows. kissing each ear of maize
they find, making the sign of the Cross.
He enters the only street of a village with a victory cry.
All dismount, tie up at a hitching-post
outside a cantina. One goes to check it out.
—*Crouch down*, the other says, *Assassins go for a head-shot.*
Leon stiffens looking along a roofline of storefronts:
—*So even should I survive, my brain...*
The guard inside beckons Leon into the cantina.
He sits in a corner, his back protected by two walls.
A squat balding man in white apron notes the pistols
with no surprise. Leon holds up one finger:—*Tequila.*
The guard at the door grunts:
—*There's a big man coming across the street.*
The big man looks over swinging doors,
the guard blocks the door:—*Closed, private party...*
—*I have an important message for Señor Trotsky*
Leon recognizes the voice:—*Let him in.*
Diego walks to Leon's table:—*I don't know*
how to say this...Your son, Lev, he...died...
yesterday in a Paris hospital.
Leon's face becomes a mask of ashes and snow.
He lowers his head to his arms on table:
—*My son! Stalin has murdered my son!* he sobs.

Diego touches Leon's arm:—*Lo siento, Leon…*
Trotsky bats Diego's hand away without looking up.
The bodyguards reach for their .45s
Diego stares them down:—*Relax*
—*Ah, poor Natalia, she shouldn't have to suffer this alone.*
Can we get back to Mexico City right away, Schussler?
—*My car's parked right outside,* Diego offers.
Leon chokes, trying to clear his throat:—*All right.*
           It's quicker than going back to Patzcuaro.
Leon, Rivera, and Schussler pile into the station wagon.
The other guard begins roping the horses together.
—*Ivan the Terrible,* Leon mumbles.
—*What?*
—*Before you kill the man himself, kill everyone around him.*
By the time you're tired of tormenting him, his soul
is dead. He will lift his chin to your blade.
Leon stares blankly, chewing his words:
Diego, get as far as possible from me.
People close to me turn up dead.
Diego accelerates up the hill,
throwing up a wake of golden dust.

Mourning

Natalia looks at Leon's face,
and faints to the floor. He kneels,
cradling her head, kissing her fine silver hair.
Her eyes at last open…no words.
He lifts her to the day bed:—*We are without a future.*
Through windows, flecks of white light
off leaves, snow falling in the Valley of Mexico,
a statue of Tlaloc in the garden becomes his
father in Persian wool hat entering the bedroom,
his mouth forming five inaudible words.
Bulblight in the bedroom brightens
to a blinding glare. Leon rocks Natalia
davining like a catatonic. In her hair he sees
snow swirled in a glass globe, the words Mother,
Grave sift illegibly past the window in a river of wind.
He stares into a darkness black as crows' wings
inside him, down to the bones.
There, in a sphere of candle-light, a boy reading a book
                    Pushkin's Poetry.
Dawn   Noon   Evening   Night   Dawn
A yeshiva boy in snapshots each year as he turns into a man
grows a goatee, his face on posters, fist raised
above a crowd, he in military uniform in a railcar
as it steams through the Urals, Frida's voice echoing
in the rhythm of the rails:—*The person inside your person
person never never was you, was you, was it, Leon?*
He shouting at Stalin in the Kremlin:
—*You are the gravedigger of the Revolution!*
daylight, dark, daylight, dark…so fast it becomes
the moving picture of timelessness.

Predawn of an indeterminate day,
he sees a speck of light grow into the face of his son, Lev.
Beneath is Leon's own, abstract, eyeless,
made of chrome, glass, the statue Diego might have sculpted.
—*I want to go home, I want to see my mother's grave.*
Natalia touches his cheek:—*That is death.*
In her eyes a small rail station lit by torches…
Remember when the soldiers came to send us into exile?
How Lev shouted on the railway platform,
Save Trotsky! Save the Hero of the Revolution!
—*Everything was shadows, and snow…*
He kisses her hand: *At least we have not betrayed one another…*
—*Please, no denials, Leon, that would be too horrible.*
He sees two convex Fridas reflected in Natalia's irises:
—*Yes, I imagined a sexual conquest, but that's not what happened.*
    I am your old faithful dog, Nata.
She begins to weep:—*Oh, can we save Sergei from Stalin?*
—*Perhaps, if I were to die…*
—*That's Stalin's insane logic! You must live*
to go on fighting… for humanity's sake, for Lev's sake.
—*I have found, in a darkness within me I never knew existed,*
that my grief for Lev is my own, I won't share it, it is mine,
as I, finally, am mine. There is no communism of grief.
Natalia grasped his shoulder—*What are you talking?*
—*All the — isms , including Trotskyism,*
are destined for the ash heap of history, Nata.
He stands, begins to pace… *I want to bring Seva here.*
—*But will Jeanne give him up?*
—*She has no rights in the matter, we are his blood.*
A knock:—*Leave us alone!* Natalia cries.
Diego's voice through the door:—*There's a gang of reporters.*
They want a statement. Natalia opens the door.
A crowd of reporters:—*You've been acquitted! Any comment?*
Over his shoulder, Leon barks:—*Meaningless!*

Noche de Ninos Muertos

Darkness, the sound of creaking oarlocks,
an hourglass lantern swinging on a prow hook
rocked by a lone boatman.   In the distance
a small island in Lake Patzcuaro, Janitzio,
a town crowned by an adobe church,
as smoothly rounded as a bleached skull
a town, a humped belly of white-fish houses
stuck in the one pin-cushion hill, a tiara of lit candles
wavering like moonlight through rubies.
Diego, Frida, Leon, Natalia, André Breton, Angelina
disembark onto a creaking dock, disappear into
the yellow wax glow of a cemetery crowning
the hill.   Marimba music, a thousand votary candles
in cups, brilliant silver light. The man
playing the marimba uses human shin bones for hammers.
Leon watches an aging couple carrying
the beragged corpse of their daughter,
seating her skeleton at a picnic table set with food,
offering her wine-sopped bread.
Leon leans to Diego:—*What're they saying?*
—*Family business. Births. They don't have to mention deaths,
the dead know the dead. Marriages, the usual…
how the fishing's going.*
Skulls, masks of skulls, a skelton in tuxedo, top hat,
a skeleton in Bishop's robes, mitre, kisses the tuxedo.
Leon looks at another mausoleum,
sees himself and Natalia carrying Lev's corpse,
by shoulders and knees, clad in his best blue serge suit,
seating him at a metal fold-out picnic table.
Leon tears a loaf of black bread, offers a handful to Lev:

—My son, you probably want to know
how goes the struggle. We're inching along
The world is drawing its breath in for a long siege...
     Lev, tell me, Is there a God?
Lev's face, cheeks gone, nose gone,
scraps of skin still clinging to his forehead.
Leon turns away in time to see André
palm a small ceremonial bowl from a headstone:
—What're you doing?
André pocketing the bowl:—A man should have what he loves.
—At the expense of these poor people?
—Don't be so bourgeois, Leon.
Leon waves Breton off in an Ah, go on, gesture
then:—*It's over, whatever there was.*
          End of conversation!
He turns away from Breton, faces Diego.
Come, translate for me, teach me the idiom
Diego says—*In the beginning,*
En el comienzo... es la palabra... say it...
—En el comienzo... Leon echoes... *es la palabra...*

Dream of Lubienka

Interior: the cubic geometry of an interrogation room
lit by one bare lightbulb. No table, chairs, only
padded walls, a windowless door.
Two men in prison uniforms sit on the floor,
backs against the wall, faces bruised,
eyes swollen, lips split.
Through water-stained walls, Leon and Diego step.
Diego looks around the room: —*What is this place?*
—*Hell, without the metaphysics…*
—*These are not men, they are dust stuck together with spit.*
—*One is Zinoviev, one is my brother-in-law, Kamenov,*
    my sometime friends…
—*Did you have a falling-out?*
—*It began the night after Kerensky's fall…*
they came to my office, in jovial moods, to celebrate,
    to invite me for cigars and cognac.
—*You turned them down?*
—*Worse, I chastised them. "Cigars? Cognac?*
while our comrades starve in the streets of St. Petersburg!"
What an imperious prig I was.
By turning on them, I gave Stalin
the chance he needed to form a trioka with these two.
Together they ousted me from the Politburo.
From there it was all dowward to these dark regions.
The door opens by the hand of a uniformed woman:
Josef Stalin walks into the room.
Zinoviev and Kamenov try to stand.
Stalin smooths his moustache, looks both men up and down:
—*One of you will walk out of here this very night…*
Diego pulls on Leon's sleeve:

—*What's he saying, Leon? I don't speak Russian.*
Leon answers: —*Kamenov is croaking, "I admit I harbored thoughts…"*
and Stailin says in his typical crude way,
"Come, come, spare me the bullshit…"
Leon holds his head between both hands.
Stalin turns to Zinoviev: —*What have you to say?*
Leon shouts: —*Don't say anything!*
   Don't give him the satisfaction!
Zinoviev can not hear: —*Kamenov gave the order*
   to have you shot as you left the Kremlin…
—*But your bunglers only wounded my double.*
Zinoviev spits through his teeth: —*You said one of us…*
Stalin laughs in his face: —*Do you think I'd let*
a couple of Jew boys off the hook? No, I only wanted
proof that all men are rotten cowards who deserve to die…
Leon rushes Stalin, swinging his fists,
but they pass through. His arms drop by his sides:
He turns to Diego: —*I wrote Kamenov two months ago,*
to pack up his family and get out of Russia
but he wouldn't listen, nobody listens!
Diego pulls Leon back through the wall.

Diego Voice-Over: Mirror of the Night

Diego crouches behind cargo boxes, spying on
a luxury liner, *The Columbus*, gold letters on white prow
moored by thick cabled rope. Kleig-lights. Diego:
O little drop of Jewish blood coursing through my veins,
if I'm only a man as Frida says with my brains between
my legs, why am I waiting in a gray gauze of fog on
the docks watching this ship take on freight? It would
make more sense if I were waiting for a woman. Even now
I see her hem raised, she, bent back over a bathroom
sink, her vulva liquid, glistening, her blood flaring like
phosphorous, both of us burning, our cells lightlless fires
that gutter and are gone. Yet if for me life is one endless
night of neon hotels, sneaking around using creepy
bellhops to cover my tracks, then how am I able to paint
young people watching the rich through big magnifying
lenses with their fancy drugs? They are only dying,
and I must use a thin wash of watercolor to show how
I see they're ghosts. Forget the politics or the reasons
we give. The ship's captain leans on his quarterdeck,
cigar in teeth, as two torpedos with swastikas get
lowered into the hold like a snake with two penises.
Silent in hurraches, I climb stacked boxes to a warehouse
roof, an electrical hum inside, my eyes wide, as
Wehrmacht helmets march by, boots of soldiers clop
like hooves. Guard dogs snuffle. What damage they
will do to my face, which is, as Frida says, a 'mirror of
night,' if they catch me, O drop of Jewish blood? To
see row upon row, under tarpulin, barrels of oil
earmarked for the Fatherland No, I am here to listen
for the voices of caged men, women, children, muffled,

crying Bitte! inside wooden crates. Where can I take
my suspicions? El Presidente? He's in on it. We all are.
We who desire. Diego climbs down off the roof,
gets into his car, drives away, headlights off.

Transplanting Cactus

On the north shore of Lake Chapala,
Leon and Diego dig a maguey out of hard-pan.
They are seen from ground-level,
framed against an oil-drilling operation noisily going on
two hundred yards away; pumping up and down,
the workmen in hard hats
slinging long chains, making up pipe.
The bodyguards lean on Diego's station wagon,
smoking and joking. Leon swings a pick,
Diego shovels dirt onto a ridge like a circular grave.
—*Take care or you'll strike the roots,* Diego warns.
Leon stops to wipe his brow with a blue bandana.
—*When do we get to the bottom of this?*
Diego smiles: —*We'll sooner fathom the mystery of love.*
The drilling machine clanks as its pipe spins.
In the sky, a red-tailed hawk silently spirals on a thermal.
—*So we must dig to China?*
—*You're becoming more Mexican every day, Leon.*
Leon resumes hacking with the pick, bits of mica fly.
Diego motions to Schussler to bring water.
Schussler hands it to him; he drinks from the water bag:
—*Frida is helping me finish Paulette's portrait.*
—*She doesn't mind?*
—*Of course she minds, I'd be wounded if she didn't mind.*
Trotsky drinks: —*You're quite the Casanova.*
—*You have no idea.*
The roots lie exposed, long white filaments of jellyfish.
Leon rocks the maguey back and forth, roots
creaking rhythmically, giving off an almost-human cry.

—I believe Stalin had Lenin poisoned... he looks to gauge Diego's reaction.

Diego rocks the maguey; it gives, comes loose out of the ground.

—I believe Cardeñas is selling oil to Hitler.

As a Jew you must see the horror...

—I'm not a Jew, I'm a revolutionary...

Leon grunts as he lifts to wrap roots in burlap.

Diego pours water on the roots: *—I'm starting a new political party.*

—What about the Fourth International?

—Why did you kick me off the Pan American Committee?

—Diego, Diego, Leon sings like a peasant, *why be a petty functionary?*

—You have no respect for me...

—Every time I stand before one of your murals I'm in awe.

Diego sneers:*—What about me? Is it because I'm a Mexican?*

—You're a man of fantastic imagination!

The hawk in the distance plunges to the ground,

rises again, flapping its wings, a long snake in its talons.

Diego rolls down his sleeves:*—I'm going to denounce Cardeñas in the press.*

Leon holds his chest as if he's just taken a .45 slug in the heart,

slumps onto the circular dirt pile:*—Why would you do that?*

—For you!

Leon looks down:*—You have dug my grave,* he whispers.

It's time Natalia and I moved out of your house.

You might as well be Stalin's best friend.

—I'd rather have many intelligent enemies than one stupid friend.

Leon looks in Diego's eyes:*—Out with it!*

—You had an affair with my wife...

—Do you really believe that?

—Are you going to deny it!

If so, you're not the man I thought you were.

Leon waves Diego off with the back of his hand:

—Goodbye then.

Diego walks to his station wagon, jumps in, roars off.

The bodyguards yell: *—Hey! Don't just leave us here!*

In the hole, surrounded by piled up dirt

Leon lies on his back, watching a long cloud,
its edges, wispy, feathery, pass through the sun
that turns into a white disk as shadows darken the land.
In a sudden dusty wind, he gathers his collar around his neck.
The oil derrick in the distance roars and rumbles.
The workmen scatter as oil blows out of the rigging.

Dress Rehearsal

Rain blares from the bell of a black sky,
drenches sidewalks, jacaranda-covered walls,
palmetto fronds flash like silver spears in gusts,
turning everything a darker shade of itself,
even the light from a second-story apartment
as it pulses down in sheets on Vienna Street.
A hand-cranked victrola pours guitar music out
on the open balcony, its hand-painted horn,
a huge pink morning glory. A young woman
dances past glass doors, in her teeth a stalk of celery
in a parody of flamenco and Andalusian passion.
David Siqueiros in trench coat dances toward her
clapping his hands on upbeat:—*Ah, those eyes!*
two fingers raised to his head like a bull's horns,
he feigns a charge as the song ends in the scratch-
scratch of the phonograph needle. A ring of men
around them on chairs. Only Siqueiros stands:
—*I've brought you here for an affair of exceptional importance…*
We're going to attack Trotsky's house!
A man hands Siqueiros a wine skin: —*At last!*
—*For me, it's personal…you remember how badly*
things were going for the Republican Army in Spain.
But we could have won if all the brigades had pulled together.
The day of battle came, and where were Trotsky's men?
He trucked them to Barcelona for a coup!
—*That bastard!*
—*I lost many friends that day, and why?*
Because Trotsky would rather Franco win than Stalin.
He squeezes a long stream of wine into his mouth.
Now this traitor enjoys the hospitality of Mexico…

Siqueiros leaves the room,
returning with a box of military uniforms:
—*The curtain is about to rise, gentlemen.*
The men tear the box apart in a game of dress-up.
Luis Arenal asks:—*How do we get inside the compound?*
Siqueiros answers:—*The gate-keeper is young and full of vinegar.*
When Julia knocks, promising a night of love, he will open.
—*Then what?* Luis continues.
—*We hunt through the compound, find Trotsky,*
and fill him full of holes… What do we want, men?
—*A dead Trotsky!*
Outside, rain continues to blacken a statue of Tlaloc
facing the street where an indio woman,
her face covered in a blue rebozo,
calls in the night for her lost children.
A transformer shoots sparks.
All the streetlamps blow out,
showers of white phosphorous like roman candles.
Every house on Vienna Street looms
like a black hill of elemental mud.

Night of the Assassins

The house on Vienna Street is lit
by floodlights the color of swamp fog.
Two black sedans pull up to its arched gates.
Six men in uniform step out with automatic weapons.
Siqueiros walks to guardhouse:—*Snap inspection!*
he shout at two dozing policemen.
They squint into flashlight beams,
then step outside, buttoning their tunics.
Nestor and Mateo knock them both out with pistol butts.
Siqueiros rings the gate bell, then steps aside.
A young man opens the peep-hole.
Julia steps up:—*It's me, Roberto, open up.*
He unlocks the gate, the men burst in at gunpoint,
one hustles Roberto to the car, locks him in the trunk.
Other men spread out through garden.
Siqueiros raises his arms, the wings of his Major's cape open.
Bursts of machine-gun fire flash like brain fever.
Bullets rend Leon's rabbits to bloody pulp.
Siqueiros sees a man standing inside a bedroom, fires.
The man stands there as bullets ricochette off walls.
—Look, men! the son of a bitch wants to die!
We've got to get the book he's writing about Stalin!
Two men hurl thermos bombs,
metal canisters clanging as they hit adobe walls.
Siqueiros sees the man drop to floor.
From a pill—box atop the walls, return fire rattles,
tracer bullets whiz, a shrill shriek inside the house.
The distant two—throated wail of police sirens.
Siqueiros blows his whistle,
a dozen men pile into two cars like a circus act,
fish-tailing down the rain-slicked street.

The Smoke Clears

Red lights of squad cars swing through carbide
fog like smeared lipstick. The first birds of morning
pipe up the smoking aftermath. Rainwater
gushes from spouts as Colonel Salazar enters
the walled garden, his open trenchcoat flapping,
his trusty "bloodhounds," Galindo and Estrada,
survey the swiss-cheesed house. Uniformed police
poke through debris in Leon's office, his desk
littered with spent bullets on unfinished manuscripts.
Shattered French windows grin like broken teeth
in a drunkard's head, the bedroom doorway
steel like a submarine bulkhead, bullet holes crater
walls, plaster chips on the floor like scabs,
sheets of paper swirl in the wind,
dancing like white ghosts. Leon and Natalia in
pajamas enter, carrying Seva, bleeding from a leg wound;
they lay him on a day-bed covered with a serape
woven with the colors of dawn.
—*Call an ambulance!* Salazar orders.
He turns to Estrada:—*Find the so-called bodyguards.*
Galindo and Estrada disappear through the same door.
Leon, Natalia stroke the boy's blond hair.
—*Well?* Salazar asks, lighting a cigarette.
—*Natalia and I were shocked awake by machine-gun fire.*
Natalia asks Leon:—*Why did you just stand there?*
—*I had to protect my archives.*
Salazar huffs: —*I warned you this would happen
if you moved to this tarpaper shack of an undefendable house.*
—*Poor Seva,* Leon coos, ignoring Salazar.
Estrada pushes Robins, Schussler into the study.

Salazar sneers:—*And you call yourselves professionals?*
The ex-United States Marines stand silent, handcuffed by shame.
Robins answers:—*This kid Harte let them through.*
—*Where is he?*
An ambulance siren sounds in the near distance
—*He's gone,* Schussler says, *maybe he was in with them.*
—*And what's your story?*
—*My weapon jammed...*
—*I'll question you two at El Pocito.*
Salazar, Galindo and Estrada step aside, huddle:
—*Looks like an inside job, the whole thing, staged.*
Salazar turns to Leon: —*Did you recognize anyone?*
—*Josef Stalin.*
—*Anyone more immediate?*
—*Arrest the entire leadership of the Mexican Communist Party.*
—*Get serious. You know I can't do that.*
A young medical intern pushes his way through the police,
kneels, examines Seva's wound. Two attendants
place Seva on a stretcher.
—*Will you come to the hospital, grandfather?*
Leon kisses his cheek:—*As soon as I can.*
Salazar announces:—*I'm going to investigate a certain local painter.*
—*Not Diego, he's my friend.*
—*Not anymore,* Salazar says. *Did you read his attack on Cardeñas?*
—*It was not an attack on me.*
—*Go to Rivera's house,* Salazar orders, *bring him in.*
He turns to see Leon's reaction.
Leon is twenty feet away, stooping, chasing his archives,
the report that Stalin ordered a pharmacist,
with a Capuchin knowledge of poisons,
be assigned to Lenin.
As Leon chases these bits of paper
blown from cactus thorn to flower bush,
he sees his bloody dead white rabbits:—*O, God!* he cries.

Getaway

Diego watches sun rise through his studio window,
sees two men in trenchcoats walking up street
on their way to work. He stretches,
puts a pot of water on his hot plate.
The phone rings:—*It's me,* Paulette's voice whispers.
        I'm in the hotel across the street.
—*Are you coming over? I'm in the mood.*
—*Don't talk, listen. There's two plainclothes dicks
packing heaters snooping around your house.
We better scram before they slam you in the hoosegow.*
He puts down the receiver, opens a closet,
takes out a suitcase, and as he starts throwing clothes in it,
Paulette taps on his back door.
—*You are amazing...* he starts to say.
She puts her finger over his lips:
—*I'll get the car started.*
Diego hands her the car keys,
she takes her portrait under arm, goes to the staircase.
—*I can't believe you're doing this...*
She winks: —*It'll be fun, being on the lam together.*
When he hears her turn the engine over he sneaks down,
tea kettle whistling as a decoy. He slips into the back,
covers himself with the portrait.
She drops the car in reverse: a small high-pitched animal cry!
Diego bursts up from under painting to see.
There, on the driveway as Paulette corners onto the street
wheels squealing, Fulang the monkey writhes in pain.
Galindo and Estrada shout:—*Stop!*
bam! bam! shots fired over the car. He collapses back
under the canvas crying:—*Fulang, poor Fulang!*

Paulette shouts over her shoulder —*Where are we headed!*
—*North, to Guanajuato, Antonia will hide us.*
—*Ah, yes, the witch...*
As Paulette guns it past the shop fronts of San Angel
Diego climbs into the front seat.
...What's this all about, Diego?
—*I discovered a German luxury liner loading Mexican oil for U—boats.*
    Cardeñas will have me killed to keep his secret.
—*So I'm in an international espionage case?*
—*Don't you read the papers?*
—*I'm down here on vacation from a movie Charlie's making*
called "The Great Dictator." I play a girl in the ghetto.
Goon squads come to smash windows but I'm not afraid,
        I brain them with a frying pan.
Paulette sees drops of sweat roll down Diego's face,
eyes fevered:—*Are you ill?*
Diego mutters:—*Fulang is...was, much more than a pet monkey.*
Diego turns his face toward the passenger-side window,
sees a reflection of Paulette at the wheel
her jaw set, her eyes flashing.
Chapultepec eucalyptus trees glow in pink dawn light.
He slumps, pointing north, up the Paseo.
The golden Angel of Independence watches
Paulette gunning it around the rotary
from her perch fifty feet above the ground.

Guanajuato

In the hills above Guanajuato,
Diego points Paulette down a dirt road.
The car slashes through the rain puddles,
pigeons startle up through the ruined towers
of an abandoned church. Paulette stops the car,
runs down a muddy path, reappears with Antonia.
They each hoist him under his armpits
and help him to a hut, lay him down
on a straw mat inside. A brasero throws
bits of light into darkness, twists of herbs,
thatched sticks hanging down from rafters.
Firelight gleams in Diego's red eyes.
Antonia turns to Paulette:—*Is he sick or is he cursed?*
—*I ran over his monkey this morning.*
—*Ai! Pobre Fulang!* Antonia shouts, *Pobre Diego!*
—*What's this thing between Diego and the monkey?*
—*La cabeza,* Diego groans.
Antonia crouches through doorway into the rain.
Paulette wipes Diego's forehead:—*Poor giant baby.*
Antonia ducks back into hut, soaking wet, arms muddy,
carrying a burlap bundle the size of an earthen jug:
—*Lord Tlaloc,* she chants, *help me cure Diego.*
Crickets chirp, treefrogs creak…
ore crushing machines at the Valenciana mine throb.
Antonia pulls down a dried monkey skin from rafters,
rubs Diego's head with its pelt, her face
gleaming firelight, daubs of gold,
indigo from the Virgin of Guadelupe's nimbus of swords.
She holds an egg between her hands to warm it,
punctures both ends with a darning needle

hands it to Diego… he sucks the yolk down.
She turns to the brasero, throws the shell into the fire,
chanting *Tlaloc, Tlaloc…*
She turns to Paulette:—*I am the one.*
I shared the vision of the ghost at the well.
Paulette looks at Antonia:—*This is making me crazy!*
What well, what ghost, what are you talking about?
—*It was I who found the silver the Riveras used*
to move to Mexico City where the viper, Frida, lived.
—*Does Diego know you think of his ex-wife that way?*
—*I have always known she would bring him to grief.*
Paulette continues wiping Diego's brow:—*He still loves her.*
—*Of course, Tlaloc's truths always come in opposites.*
The great—how do you say, mentiroso… is the most faithful.

Close Iris   Open Iris
Paulette and Diego in the Guadalajara airport terminal
Outside a DC3's engine starts, blue smoke jetting from engines.
Paulette asks: —*What was in Antonia's bundle?*
—*You don't want to know.*
Salazar, Galindo, and Estrada walk up to Diego and Paulette:
—*Come with me, and quietly,* Salazar says.
—*What of my friend?* Diego asks.
Salazar waves his hand: —*She can go back to Los Angeles.*
Diego gets up, turns to Paulette, puts the portrait into her hands.
—*Go make your movie with Charlie… Don't worry, kid,*
        they can't pin nuthin' on me.
Salazar points to a cyclopean bird in the painting:
—*What's this?*
—*The sign of my perversity.*
Paulette walks toward roaring airplane
carrying the painting, looks back through the prop wash,
sees her reflection on the plate glass and through it
Diego being handcuffed.

Actor Without a Script

A hotel room on a sweltering August afternoon.
Above the bed's headboard a cheap painting—
men ladling juice from maguey plants with long-handled dippers.
Sylvia stands in Frank's pajama top, her buttocks bare,
staring in a dresser mirror,
bending her nose with her finger:
—*They say plastic surgeons work miracles these days…*
She slides into bed next to the man she calls Jacques.
He lies there, propped by pillows, smoking a cigarette.
… I can't believe things are back to normal at the Trotskys.'
—*Make a fist, Sylvia, hold it like that.*
She holds the fist a minute:—*It's starting to go numb.*
—*Exactly.* Frank crushes out his cigarette.
—*So, you're saying, even if the guards wanted to keep vigilant…*
She takes his hand, places it on her thigh:—*You're so smart.*
—*Did you ask the Old Man if he'd read my article?*
She winds his hair with her fingers:—*Don't worry.*
Frank sits up in bed, flicking his lighter:
—*That would mean a lot to me.*
She slides her hand over his bare chest,
he rolls away, lighting another cigarette:
—*It hurts when you lord it over me.*
You're the secretary of the most famous political exile in the world,
and I'm nothing, just another greedy businessman…
Sylvia gets up on her knees:
—*The last thing I want is to hurt your feelings,*
        arouse them is more like it…
—*Then get me in to see the old man.*
He walks his two fingers down her cleavage to her belly.
She leans back, letting her hair dangle behind her,

kisses him hard, rolls over, straddles his hips:
—*Where are the riches you've stolen from the poor, capitalist pig?*
—*Where revolutionary scum like you will never find it!*
She grinds her hips into him:
—*You arrogant bastards must be stood against a wall and shot!*
She slaps him, first one cheek, then another.
He thrusts his hips up into her...groans:—*Mother...of God,*
rolls her off... reaches for another cigarette,
gets up, walks to the blinds, hitching up his pajama bottoms.
Sylvia lies on the bed, exhausted, in a heap, her cheeks red:
—*Frank?*
—*What now?*
—*Remember how you used to read poetry to me?*
He lifts the blinds to look onto the street:—*That was long ago...*
—*You bought me irises on the Champs.*
—*Irises were then in bloom... and rumors of war...*
—*There's going to be hell to pay, and we'll be lucky if we survive...*
—*Who wants to survive?*
She gets up on one arm, looks at Frank staring out the window:
—*Whatever can you be thinking?*
—*How my mother used to read "Jack and the Beanstalk" to me,*
how Jack outwits the giant. I'm thinking,
She must've have wanted me to have magic in my life.
—*How sweet.*
—*Look, I have to go to the office...an appointment.*
—*You sound like a perfectly dreary businessman, Frank.*
—*Don't start,* he warns, slipping into his trousers.
—*Are you leading a secret life on me?*
—*Yeah, Diego's girlfriend and I meet to discuss art and revolution.*
Sylvia's eyes go flinty:—*And are her insights revealing?*
Frank pulls on a dress shirt:—*Very.*
Sylvia gets up and punches Frank in the back, hard:—*It's not funny!*
He takes her in his arms:—*I love it,* he laughs.

Blind Alley

Frank stands under a street sign:
Calle de Jesús Teran. On the next corner,
lights from a café that zzzz and crackle,
distant cab horns blare through
an accordion playing "Guadalajara."
As Frank walks closer, he sees a man
seated on an orange crate, wearing dark glasses
canting his head back and forth as he speaks:
—*How are you this evening, Ramon?*
Frank sees the musician is blind:
—*How did you know it was me?*
—*I hear something in the way a gringo walks,*
something bold, not quite stealthy, something
you will have to fix if you are to succeed in the mission.
—*Are you the one I'm supposed to meet?*
—*I am if you are ready to strike the blow.*
—*Who could ever be ready for such a thing?*
—*Let me tell you a story: The new curate up the hill*
was visited one night in his rectory by a man who said,
'There is an Aztec treasure buried beneath your cemetery.'
—*Stories of Aztec treasure are common.*
—*What is uncommon is that after the man left*
the priest inquired with his parishioners who said
        the man had died two years before.
—*And your point?*
—*That the dead walk among us.*
You will help Leon awaken from the dream of life…
—*I'll think of that when the moment comes… if it comes.*
—*He wants you to enter his house. He is oh-so weary*
like Moctezuma inviting Cortés into his palace

since, after all, he was a magical being-what you
in Europe would call a centaur…
—*Look, I can't stand here for a history lesson.*
—*But just as Cortés entered Moctezuma's house*
by the hand of his serving woman, his Malinche,
so you will enter the foreigner's house
with the aid of your Sylvia and you will aim your
weapon at his head which is a sarcophagus
filled with putrefying human flesh…
   Do you see my instrument case?
—*Yes*
—*Take it with you.*
Frank tries to lift it, grunts from the weight of it:
—*What's in here?*
—*A typewriter. With it you will compose a letter*
explaining your motives in taking el Viejo's life…
—*And they are?*
—*You are a naïve idealist, attracted to his politics,*
but you are utterly destroyed when he asks you
to travel to Moscow and kill Stalin…
—*… which he is already charged with, right?*
—*Is there a tune you'd like to hear, Ramon?*
—*Do you know 'Show me the way to go home'?*
The blind accordion player chuckles at Frank's little joke,
but begins to play the old Vaudeville favorite.
—*Also, you are horrified when Trotsky requires you*
to give up the woman you love for the sake of his evil plan.
You take history into your own hands…
—*I'm no history-maker…*
—*You want to see your mother again, don't you?*
—*Tell Isaak to let her go! Then we'll talk about making history…*
The blind man resumes playing his accordion, singing
—*Later, when the deed is done,*
   and the race is practically run…
Oh, and another thing, the Aztec treasure is buried right here,

under my feet, along the old causeway that led
from the temples of Tenochtitlán to the mainland
that night, that Noche de Triste... Adios, mi amigo.
The man known as Frank Jacson lifts the accordion case,
staggers down the street, disappears around a corner.

Wedding Plans

Late afternoon. The Trotsky house:
Natalia greets Sylvia and Frank on the shady terrace.
On a wrought-iron table, sliced fruit, a bowl of ice cubes,
a tea pot steaming. Sylvia in summer hat, flowered
dress, high heels. Natalia kisses her cheek.
—*When is the happy event?*
—*We're flying to New York, day after tomorrow.*
Frank watches Leon lift his new rabbits out of their hutches,
cleaning the wooden boxes with hose and brush.
—*Big wedding?*
—*A few friends from The Daily Worker.*
Natalia pours hot tea over ice:—*The reception?*
Sylvia nervously:—*Is the Ritz too decadent?*
Natalia smiles:—*It's only once.*
Frank squints to see Leon in slanted sunlight.
—*We'll honeymoon in the Alps.*
Frank's going to teach me to climb the Matterhorn.
Natalia to Frank:—*Will you continue your business in New York?*
—*I could make a few investments for you,* Frank offers.
Natalia, taken aback:—*Do you think we'd play that game?*
Sylvia kicks Frank's shin under the table:
—*It's only a joke, right, Frank?*
—*Yes, Mr. Trotsky's politics…with Wall Street money, see?*
Natalia calls: —*Come wish the happy couple bon voyage!*
Leon marches to the terrace, wiping his hands,
shaking hands with Frank:—*Have a happy life!*
—*I'll miss you,* Sylvia sniffs back a tear.
Leon embraces Sylvia, pats her hand:
—*There, there, you will always be my special girl.*
—*I'm returning tomorrow to discuss my article, right?* Frank asks.

—O, yes, I have some ideas.
Sylvia stands, leans to give Natalia a peck:*—Time to go.*
—But you've only just got here! Natalia protests.
—We must pack. A million things to do yet.
The couple walks back through the garden, out the gate.
Natalia pours tea for Leon: *—Frank said the most peculiar thing.*
He offered to play the stock market for us.
      What a strange sense of humor!
—He's harmless, a playboy who's taken an interest in politics
      just to please his fiancé…
—He looked sickly pale to me.
—He's written this jejune article on bureaucratic collectivism.
—Why help him?
—I have to trust someone. If new people can't come into my life,
      how can I influence the future?
Natalia touches his shoulder: *—You're a saint.*
—Honestly, Nata, Leon says with mock offense
as he sips his tea and the sun slips
behind the garden gate.

The Deed

Frank steps out of his cream-colored Buick.
Dust swirls rise to envelope him in August evening light,
his raincoat glittering like powdery gold wings.
Natalia sees Frank's face, white as a spark plug:
—*Why the raincoat?*
—*Mark my words, a storm is coming.*
Leon comes out on the terrace to greet Frank,
mopping his brow as he leads him into his cluttered study:
—*My friend Jesús jokes that it gets so hot in August*
    if you died and went to Hell
    you'd come back for your overcoat.
Frank isn't laughing.
Leon sits in his desk chair, begins to read his notes
on Frank's article. Frank stands behind Trotsky,
lays down his raincoat, slowly drawing out a mountaineer's ice-axe
from the pocket he's sewn into the lining.
On the victrola a string quartet strikes up a little night music.
Frank feels the heft of his ice-axe, calculates
the point of his blow. Leon speaks without looking:
—*You begin by attacking Stalin*
then the concept of leadership itself…
We're not out to destroy the people's need to believe
—*But isn't that what enslaves them?*
—*We don't want to take the magic out of the world, Mr. Jacson.*
—*Please, do me the justice of reading the whole piece…*
Leon holds up a hand in agreement, continues reading.
Frank Jacson cocks his arm. The white rabbits
in the garden blur into the manzanilla,
a bi-plane overhead bubbles in the air like mineral water.
The assassin's weapon enters the base of Leon's

skull with a *thock!* Blood gushes from the wound…
a million words fall off pages of botched treaties…
firebrand speeches, biographies, polemics, execution orders,
treatises on art and revolution, manifestoes by the dozen,
entire lexicons of armed political struggle,
letters beseeching his poorly armed partisans in Spain
to go on fighting, to forget the rain and believe
in each other, all the letters fall into gibberish
as they stream out of his head, each
seraph, the written word, in pulsing clots.
Leon swings around to face Frank,
knocks him against a large wall-map of the world.
He staggers to the doorway:—*Natalia!*
She and two guards rush into Leon's office
as he collapses across dining room floor onto small hooked rug.
Natalia cradles her husband's head in her lap.
The guards disarm, beat Frank down:
—*Don't…kill him*, Leon rasps. *Make him…talk.*
Frank's checks are mashed into pulp, black blood oozes:
—*Trust Stalin to send a masochist to a beating.*
—*They've got my mother!* Frank shouts through his bloody mask.
—*Who is 'they'?*
—*Kill the enemy, end it all*, Frank croaks.
Leon looks up into Natalia's eyes, touches his chest:
—*I feel…here…that Stalin this time has succeeded.*
He tries to touch Natalia's cheek
Tell the Fourth Internationale…to keep…
His eyes close.
—*It is not a man who dies*, Jacson says, *but an idea.*
The room dissolves in brilliant silver light.

In El Pocito

Colonel Salazar opens the interrogation room door.
Sylvia walks in, dressed for a funeral.
The man known as Frank Jacson sits at a table.
He taps his cigarette on his thumbnail:
—*Well, well, look who's here.*
—*If you love Sylvia as you say you do, show her,* Salazar urges.
—*Murderer! Liar!* Sylvia screams.
She lunges at Jacson, tearing at his eyes with her fingernails.
Jacson yells:—*Colonel, what have you done!*
Salazar steps up behind her, pulls her away.
She slumps to her knees, cry-screaming as if she'll never stop.
—*How could you, Jacques? I mean, Frank.*
O, God, I don't even know your real name.
—*By what aliases have you known him?*
—*When I first met him in Paris he was Jacques Mornard.*
He said he had to change it to Frank Jacson to escape being drafted
into the Belgian army... but even that must be a lie ...
he has no name, he is no one...
—*This man says he killed Trotsky so you two could be together.*
—*A lie,* she sobs into the floor. *Assassin!*
—*Take me out of here, I beg you, Colonel.*
Sylvia gets up, spits in Jacson's face:
—*Kill him! He doesn't deserve a trial!*
She lunges for Salazar's side-arm, pulls it from his holster,
places the gun muzzle to No Name's forehead.
Jacson shakes, his eyes roll up:—*Colonel, what have you done?*
—*Oh, what have I done? A great man*
murdered by a worm like you! But what am I...
the assassin's whore? She turns the revolver to her face
pulls the trigger with her thumbs.
Click! Click! Click!

The Urn and the Egg

Diego walks with Natalia in the garden of Leon's house,
        Natalia carries a funerary urn.
They stand beside a square brick fountain pool.
Reflected in the water, Leon's funeral cortege in slow-motion:
President Cardeñas, Natalia Sedova, Diego Rivera, Frida Kahlo
        Col. Salazar lead a funeral cortege.
A military band plays a slow Russian dirge
through crowds in mourning black, anonymous women,
weeping hysterical, tearing their *rebozos,*
the coffin on a caisson draped with the Soviet flag
clop-clop of horses' hooves on cobblestone.
As they pass the Metropolitan Cathedral
Aztec dancers in colored feathers, ankle bells jingling,
spin to the beat of native drums, and out of the Cathedral,
a procession holding up *papier maché* effigies,
the Virgin of Guadalupe, saints, angels, with golden halos…
white wings through steel bar gates, sharp as devouring teeth…
young soldiers, their eyes gleaming like oiled bayonets.
A mariachi band stands below the Mexican flag
at half mast, singing a *corrida.*
Natalia looks up at Diego, his arm around her waist,
comforting her, holding her up:—*What is that song?*
Diego translates:—*They are singing…*

>   *It was on a Tuesday evening in August*
>   *the fatal blow was struck*
>   *which has stirred our hearts to sadness*
>   *and ended Trotsky's luck…*

Close Iris   **Open Iris**
Natalia kneels and with a trowel digs beside a maguey.
—*This is the plant Leon and I dug up at Lake Chapala.*

Natalia doesn't look up, speaks as she digs:
—*I always had a bad feeling about these plants…*
     so thorny, so cruel…
When the hole is as deep as her arm, she settles the urn inside it:
—*Will my husband only be remembered*
     for the enormity of his failure?
Diego kneels beside her:— *Ask David Sigeriros that question. He knew Leon was important enough to kill. Whatever history says will be a shallow lie.*
He takes Natalia's hand… *truly a light has gone out of the world…*
—*What will you do now?*
—*Paint. It's all I've ever had. And it's enough…*
Natalia watches Diego place the painted egg in the hole with the urn.
—*It is good you have had him cremated.*
     At least he won't have to lie in a grave
       where his bones will ache for all eternity…
Besides, Diego adds, *being dead,*
Leon has something alive inside him…
So, as we say, 'For the next life!'

Bill Tremblay has six books of poetry, among them *Crying in the Cheap Seats* (University of Massachusetts Press), *Duhamel* (BOA Editions Ltd.), and most recently *Rainstorm Over the Alphabet* (Lynx House Press). He teaches in the MFA Program in Creative Writing at Colorado State University, and is the 2002 recipient of the John F. Stern Distinguished Professor Award as well as awards from the NEA, the NEH, the Fulbright Commission, Yaddo, Pushcart and inclusion in the anthology *Best American Poety 2003.*